THE
  U1

'Mary Bowmaker's excellent book covers a whole range of subjects such as dreams, out of body trips, near-death experiences, visions, numerology, survival after death, meditation, musical mediumship and angels. There is much of great interest on each and every page.'

Tony Ortzen, editor *Two Worlds*

The Reality of the Unbelievable

by

Mary Bowmaker

COURTENBEDE

Copyright © Mary Bowmaker 2016
First published in 2016 by Courtenbede
/o Loundshay Manor Cottage, Preston Bowyer
Milverton, Somerset TA4 1QF
Answerphone / fax: 01823 401527
e-mail: amolibros@aol.com
website: www.amolibros.co.uk

Distributed by Gardners Books, 1 Whittle Drive, Eastbourne,
East Sussex, BN23 6QH
Tel: +44(0)1323 521555 | Fax: +44(0)1323 521666

The right of Mary Bowmaker to be identified as the author of the work has been asserted herein in accordance with the Copyright, Designs and Patents Act 1988.

All rights reserved. This book is sold subject to the condition that it shall not, by way of trade or otherwise, be lent, resold, hired out or otherwise circulated without the publisher's prior consent in any form of binding or cover other than that in which it is published and without a similar condition including this condition being imposed on the subsequent purchaser.

British Library Cataloguing in Publication Data
A catalogue record for this book is available from the British Library.

ISBN 978-0-9554292-2-4

Typeset by Amolibros, Milverton, Somerset
This book production has been managed by Amolibros
Printed and bound by T J International Ltd, Padstow, Cornwall, UK

About the Author

A FORMER PROFESSIONAL MUSICIAN, both teacher and performer, Mary Bowmaker has always loved writing, small successes over the years encouraging and inspiring her to write her first book *A Little School on the Downs*; a record of the life and work of a headmistress and her school in Victorian England. *Is Anybody There*, and *Leaning on the Invisible* are her first two books about the paranormal.

This book is dedicated to my wonderful, darling parents

Mary and Stephen Wilton

and to

My Beloved Husband Peter R. Bowmaker

and Toby

Contents

Introduction	1
Chapter One *Setting the Scene*	4
Chapter Two *We are Two Worlds. We are spiritual beings in a physical body living in a material world.*	28
Chapter Three *Divine Transportation*	53
Chapter Four *An Awakening of Understanding*	80
Chapter Five *The Complete (Total) Self*	108
Chapter Six *Colour My World*	129
Chapter Seven *The Unbelievable Made Real*	149
References	174

Acknowledgements

My thanks to:

The Religious Experience Research Centre, otherwise known as RERC, Universtity of Wales, Lampeter, Ceredigion, whose archives of 'ordinary people, true experiences of the other side of life', might otherwise have been lost to the world, but for their extraordinary efforts.

To Jane Tatam from Amolibros, for her understanding and care and for all her unseen work as a publisher of such high standards, thank you and Amolibros for being there, Jane.

To Allan Oak, fellow passenger on the *Hurtigruten,* who kindly supplied the photographs.

To Sylvia Povey Kennedy, close friend and 'reader', always ready to bring certain points to my attention, adding her words of wisdom to my thinking. Thank you so much, Sylvia.

To Iris Wilding, medium and healer, whose sudden burst of inspiration gave me the title and therefore the theme of the chapter, 'Colour my World'. Thank you Iris, readers so much enjoyed taking part in a little experiment I tried out with them.

Radio Four, who continue to be a source of material, often adding to what I was already working on and at times leading me on to new paths (of thinking).

To my friends and acquaintances and strangers (remembering that a stranger's just a friend we don't know) who have so willingly and trustingly given me their own experiences, and which they have allowed me to publish, thank you.

To everyone who has shared with me, and allowed me to put out there into the world – into the Universe, their own special, often very personal, deep experiences, the simple words 'thank you', convey more love and meaning than you will ever know. Thank you.

Sincerely,

Mary Bowmaker

71° North Cape. The Northern Lights in all their glory, photos taken from the mail ship *Hurtigruten*, Norway – or to give them their proper name, the *Aurora Borealis*. Photographs by Allan Oak, facing page 118.

Introduction

WE ALL KNOW THAT the world, and our daily lives, are changing, and changing fast. This comes as we are now feeling the consequences of having moved into 'The Age of Aquarius', forecast centuries ago, to be an age of 'change'. It appears to be, that this will be an age, not only of 'change', however, but one of 'dramatic change'. The pope has recently spoken out, loudly and clearly, calling for all people of all faiths to come together, to save our planet from complete destruction, calling for a bold cultural revolution, to combat global warming – therefore causing climate change, blaming it (climate change), and we all know it is happening, on 'human action'. With the changes forecast for this new age, it 'is also written' that there will be a 'spiritual revolution'.

Could it be that we are going to have a 'bold cultural revolution', as called for by the pope, and running alongside it, a spiritual revolution, as forecast centuries ago? (After all, one is bound to impact on the other, as they both head in the same direction.)

Thinking particularly about the spiritual side of life (and change), could it be that one of the consequences of this change is the way we openly 'talk about', and try to explain, experiences of the so-called, paranormal? The word 'paranormal' now, in this new age, is rapidly changing from 'paranormal' to natural phenomena.

Natural phenomena, happening in 'experiences', multi-faceted as they sometimes are, cannot be 'easily' put into one category, therefore, we often touch on more than one experience, within an experience! There are fantastic stories out there (some of them are in this book), the other side of life making its presence felt, just waiting to be heard. Could it be that part of the proof, if we really are now at the start of the spiritual revolution, lies in the fact that fewer and fewer of us use the expression, 'Oh I don't believe in anything like that,' (referring to the paranormal) or 'no, too much for me'? Yet, hesitantly, go on to say, 'But – there – was – one – thing.'

With regard to spirituality, we have already made changes in so many seemingly 'simple' ways, but all adding up to the 'fact' of change. So many now seek alternative therapies, such as healing, both 'spiritual' and 'energy' healing, meditation, reading books and magazines on spirituality, sending out 'thoughts' for others, 'thoughts' of course, another word for 'prayer'; not that this has not been done in the past, of course it has, but done in an entirely different way of, shall we say, 'thinking'. Many of us still love to go to church and are members of the congregation, and many of us love to go and light a candle, or maybe to place flowers. Sending any thoughts or 'worries' 'out to the universe' is now perhaps, the language of a new kind of 'spirituality', the meaning of which, however, to be 'spiritual', to 'care', is just the same.

Paranormal experiences (natural phenomena), along with other changes in life that we are witnessing, are now gradually accepted as a natural part of living. Just as this is happening, it also appears to be that more of us are realising, are seeing, the magical way our lives can be transformed when we are in touch with, the 'Universe', the 'Unnamed Something', 'Creator', 'God'. Together we share the human experience, and now, together, in this new Aquarian Age, we will share the spiritual, as we embark, or continue, on the greatest adventure of all, feeling the love, the uplift, the oneness; resonating with the power, the wonder, the mystery, of being 'In Tune with the Infinite'.

Thomas, age five, chatted away as usual to what his mother called his 'imaginary friends'. Yet she stopped short in her tracks as, passing the open door to the living room where he was sitting, alone, legs astride, rolling a ball across the carpet, she was just in time to see it rolled back!

Chapter One

Setting the Scene

> 'Or ever the silver cord be loosed, or the golden bowl be broken, or the pitcher be broken at the fountain, or the wheel broken at the cistern. Then shall the dust return to the earth as it was: and the spirit shall return unto God who gave it.'
>
> *Eccles 12 – 6-7*

FASCINATING STORIES, EXCITING, UPLIFTING, perhaps unbelievable, sometimes sad; experiences of the so-called 'paranormal' (some of which are here recorded in this book) are happening every moment of life, somewhere, just as they always have, the difference being that we are now not 'shy' of telling them. For this is The New Age, the Age of Aquarius, a time for change with a capital 'C', and a feature of which is 'openness' in all areas of life; financial, social, political, religion. Openness, where we are not afraid to talk about our dreams, or an intuition, a feeling, that very special experience, or when we have seen an 'angel'. It is an age where we are encouraged to express our 'individuality', and pursue our 'self-expression', as found in the Arts: music, painting, theatre, literature, bringing forward any talents we may have. These finer points lead to and help us as we, perhaps unwittingly, become part of the Spiritual Revolution – which is a major part of the forecast, bound to happen in this new, great, age; Aquarius.

It was 1931, and Maggie Smith, a nineteen-year-old night nurse in a hospital, had an experience that would stay with her for the rest of her life. Maggie was assigned to sit with a patient who was dying. The ward was quiet, with only a shaded night-light, but enough to be able to attend to the patients' needs, and so she settled down, knowing she would be officially off duty at 3.00 a.m. Much to her annoyance, however, as she later recalled, the patient died at 2.30 a.m. so she decided to report the death at nearer to 3.00 a.m. to save herself some work. It was then that she saw a strange thing happen.

'About 2.50 a.m. I saw another body hovering above the dead body. Complete in length, thickness and contour, except that it was translucent. This I saw very clearly. In my ignorance, I thought it was the body cooling down but when it moved, undulating towards the foot of the bed I began to think about it.'

Maggie realised she had seen the spirit depart from the body, and recorded that she was not dreaming, and she was not afraid.[1]

For as long as can be remembered, nurses in hospitals, or those caring for the 'about to depart', were encouraged to leave a window open so that the spirit body, once let loose from the physical body, could slip away unhindered to the 'after-life', the world of spirit. As with a newly born baby on entering our world, the umbilical cord, connecting the baby to the mother, is severed, so it is that the 'spirit body', finally released from the 'physical body' by the severing of the 'silver cord', occurs at the time of (so-called) death. The silver cord…slowly, gradually, thinning as it pulls away from the physical; elastic, a life thread, a gossamer-like substance floating; gradually weakening, fainter, silently releasing its hold, until at last, freed from the body, the spirit enters the spirit world, now, already, a citizen of heaven.

(The old carol, 'O Come all ye Faithful', is only one example of many references to the 'citizens of heaven'.)

The silver cord, our heavenly link while here on the earth plane, fluctuates, vibrating with every pulsation of the body. There, sensitive to all our physical endeavours and emotions; and while we sleep, the silver cord enables us to leave the body, to travel in the sleep state, taking us, in our spirit body, to 'far-away places', and even, at times, to the spirit world itself...while the physical sinks ever deeper into a blissful, rejuvenating sleep.

Perhaps simply resting, lying a few inches above the physical, or returning from 'who knows where' (do *you* remember your dream/visions?), the spirit, gently guided back to the body by means of the silver cord, slips effortlessly, and gently, back into place. Unless, as sometimes happens, we have been startled into a 'rude awakening', then the spirit's return will not be smooth, but perhaps upsetting. We might experience the awful feeling of falling. In a free fall, where we never reach the bottom, but wake up in a merger of mixed emotions and vibrations, not knowing where (on earth?) we are. But usually, the move from astral travelling (as it is known) in the sleep state – the silver cord allowing us free reign to travel at will – to our return is light and pleasant, and one of which we have no recollection.

It is 'believed' by some, that the silver cord, mirroring our physical state, will become thinner and dull if we are unwell, in a poor state of health, and the (unexplained?) weight loss at the moment of death, many believe, is the removal of the 'soul/ spirit' from the body.

Maggie Smith was not astral travelling (in the sleep state), nor was she having an 'out of body' (OBE) experience, when she was privileged to witness the spirit body of her patient leave, then move away from, the physical body. Maggie Smith was a silent witness to a great, natural phenomenon, not dreaming, and not afraid.

• • •

Maureen Edwards is someone whose need to give a full and accurate account, down to the most minute detail, of affairs, from present day to the past, is impressive. Hence the value of the history/information she supplies, along with the certificates – Maureen telling us, 'I have the certificates to prove it' – as she gives the background, time and setting to the special experience she has never forgotten.

Living in London with her mother – they were true Londoners (her father was a soldier away on war service), she starts her story in 1944 when she was four years old, and a very 'poorly' child. Suffering so much, and at such a young age, was maybe why she was perhaps 'allowed' to witness…but let us think about her, try to picture her, all those years ago. A little girl with straight, fair hair, 'well made' as her mother would say; and in thinking about her, we move back, back to the '40s; the fast changing '40s, a time of shortages, rationing, and fear; fear coupled with outstanding bravery and acceptance. Here is her story.

'You ask about the illness I had when living in London. I think it was more of a chest weakness, following a bad dose of measles and whooping cough. Of course, in those days, there were no injections to prevent these conditions, and no antibiotics (not prescribed for children – only the armed forces). It was also pre NHS.'

'I remember spending a few weeks in a chest hospital in Hemel Hempstead and three months at a children's home in Broadstairs when I was only six years of age. Strangely enough, I have come across two pieces of info regarding a month's "so-called" convalescence in Brighton when I was seven years of age. All these experiences were absolutely terrible. You wouldn't think I was in the homes because I needed some rest and recuperation. The staff (all women) were cruel, strict and abusive (including a nurse at Hemel Hempstead who gave me a good smacking because I had re-arranged my bedside locker when the Matron was about to do her "rounds").

'I had to go to Great Ormond Street Hospital in London for nose washouts (a practice they no longer use as they have better remedies). These took place in wards underneath the hospital – no pictures on the walls, due to condensation, and no toys to play with. We know it was wartime, but somehow I think children were treated very third-class in those days.

'When London was going through the Blitz, we fled to some relatives in the country. I had to sleep on a bug-infested sofa and contracted impetigo. The local doctor said I needed my tonsils to be removed, so Mum took me to hospitals in Kings Lynn, Peterborough and others – I still remember being dragged around when I was feeling very unwell. All the hospitals were full with troops and were not admitting children. We eventually returned to London, but another air raid caused all the windows of our flat to be "blown out" and ceilings to come down and we had to move out for two months, whilst the landlord repaired the damage. Mum took temporary lodgings in Bicester, and the Radcliffe Old Infirmary in Oxford removed my tonsils. I remember being put into a gown and then placed in a queue of children. When I got to the front (of the queue), the anaesthetist pressed a large wad over my face – I thought I was being suffocated/murdered. This was how children were "anaesthetised" in 1944.

'Today's generation have no concept of how we kids were treated then. Unfortunately, these experiences have left deep scars.'

Now we are in 1946 and Maureen is back in London, living at 90 Alexander Road, Hornsey. On this particular night, she was 'settled' in the bed she shared with her mother, her father still away on war service. Her mother was sound asleep but Maureen believes that she, herself, was wide-awake and quite alert, as 'startled', she tried to take-in a scene being played out before her very eyes.

A small group of men in white coats, gathered together at the bottom of the bed, were engaged in some discussion or other. (Could they have been healers/doctors, from the spirit world?) As she watched, and wondered, suddenly, one of the men became aware of the little girl and turned to face her. Slowly, he made his way towards her along the left side of the bed, but at this Maureen took fright and buried herself under the clothes.

She never did tell her mother about this experience. Her parents were good people, but she had a strict (Victorian style) upbringing, and would have been accused of making up stories or telling lies, had she done so.

There was, however, one serious outcome, or repercussion from that 'visit'. From that night, through to her teenage years, Maureen started 'sleep walking'. She was witnessed by various members of the family over the years, who were both alarmed and surprised at the way she confidently wandered all over the house, even navigating her way down three steps to the basement kitchen/scullery, while at the same time, calling out the words, over and over again, 'Where are they?'

Maureen did not confide this strange tale in anyone, that is, until she met her future husband, and then only told him, after he had confided in her, his own thought-provoking 'out of body' experience…but that is another story.

• • •

In this, the twenty-first century, we have at last reached the Age of Aquarius, forecast in past centuries to be the age of a spiritual revolution and the time for humanity to return to its spiritual roots. It is the time for humanity to realise and fully understand that we are 'more than the physical body' we inhabit while here on the earth plane. It is a time when, threatened as we are (and this is happening all over the world), in all directions, and on all fronts, with problems of immense proportions while seeming to blunder our way through a mire of unending 'potential' catastrophes – We Need HELP! But close by, watching out for us, ever alert to our distresses and predicaments, the other side of life, the 'spirit world' struggles to make its presence felt. Reaching down through the darkness of our world, created by man's selfish schemes and unrelenting greed for power and possessions, the higher realms bring light in the form of hope; hope that we will 'mend our ways', see the folly of our purely materialistic aims, and change course before it is too late.

With present-day lifestyles, there is little left of what *was*, say, twenty or thirty years ago. It seems that little has been left of the fabric of life then. So much has changed, we can even think of twenty years ago as the 'olden times'. Whereas then, twenty years ago, olden times were thought of as being maybe a hundred or so years in the past; and now, although it appears that many people are no longer interested in religion in the traditional sense, people, 'we', are talking openly about 'spirit', and are no longer shy of reporting experiences. It seems that we have taken a 'jump' into another dimension of thought and attitude. (To quote a reporter in *The Sunday Times*, 'We may not be getting our spiritual fix in church anymore but if the growth of 'spirit oriented' practices like yoga are anything to go by, our hunger is greater than ever.') We need a 'living faith', that 'something' – the Universal Energy, the life force, God – *is* a proven presence in our lives, as more and more people are discovering.

'There is a rising tide of consciousness leading to a flood of understanding, an awakening; a spiritual awakening in our time; an awakening from 'the sleep of the senses' in which we mistake our bodily identity for our 'ultimate' essence'.[2]

And as we reach out to this 'presence', in love and sincerity, with a goodness of heart, gradually, we will see changes coming into our lives; openings, opportunities, occurring; happenings beyond our imagination or expectation as in the 'wonderment' of the proven presence, we witness the unbelievable made real. The unbelievable is made real in, say, a 'deeper than deep moment' we experience it as going 'within', and for whatever reason, we glimpse, feel, become aware of a 'Something'. Perhaps it might be seen as a 'personal saviour', known by whatever name, if any, we care to use, and always able to be in contact, in the form of 'open communication', if we believe in the power of 'prayer' (which is really 'thought'). Let us cultivate our extra-sensory skills, which include considering the relevance of – to name but a few – dreams, coincidence and intuition. A remarkable example of intuition recently, in March 2013, led to the discovery, in a car park in Leicester, of the bones of the Medieval King, Richard III. Following the authentication of Richard III's bones, could this discovery lead to a re-thinking of the current opinion of the king, who was much maligned throughout history, and accused of murdering the little princes in the Tower. Leading historians and archivists, working together, are now beginning to dispute the bad reputation of the king, and argue that he would be more likely to have removed them to a secret place of safety. The research continues.

• • •

Albert Einstein, scientist, is quoted as saying, 'The only real valuable thing is intuition.' Cultivate our extra-sensory skills, and never doubt our own ability to achieve the highest and the best, if we so wish to be truly human.

• • •

John had, through intuition, in one, so-called paranormal

'experience', possibly saved the life of his son who had recently moved to live and work in London. His son, another 'John', was living in an old, dilapidated flat, sharing it with his cousin who was also working in London. It was getting late on this particular night when John (the father of young John) suddenly, out of the blue – and strongly – felt there was something wrong with a gas-tap in the bedroom of the flat. Not a man to act hastily or panic, he felt the need to contact his son and warn him of the possible danger. He did this, and son John discovered that there was indeed a loose-fitting, faulty gas-tap in the bedroom.

Having had a few remarkable experiences over the years, the one that has puzzled him more than any happened when he was teaching in a special school in the north of England, and was out on a short field trip with a small class of pupils and a teacher assistant. They were only out for an hour or so, to have a wander round outside an ancient local church, and do some headstone rubbing in the old cemetery.

With the pupils happily working, John took himself for a wander over to the far part of the cemetery. As he stood, glancing around at all the ancient gravestones, he was quite 'taken aback' to see a new one, light grey in colour, on a patch of green grass, in among the old ones. Fascinated by this sight, he wandered further over to read what he knew must be something 'special', for a new grave to have a place on this hallowed, historic, site.

As he neared the place, he could read quite clearly, although still a little way away from it, the letters, set in black:

Boy Seaman
Killed in action on board the
H. M. S. Victory
Flag ship of the Admiral Lord Nelson
At the Battle of Trafalgar 1805

Astonished at what he was reading, John stood silently, reverently taking in and 'memorizing' the inscription, with something telling him 'not to move any closer'.

And as he remembers the strange feeling he had, standing there, reading the words over and over again as if to impress them on his mind, he remembered that it was now time to gather the pupils together, time for them to board the bus and head back to school.

On the way back, he told them that when they returned the next day, to finish off their work, he had something special to show them, something he had just discovered, and that they would find very interesting. That night, he could not forget what he had seen in the old cemetery and how strange he had felt, standing there. He kept going over it in his mind and thought about how clearly the words on the inscription had appeared to him, and how he had stood, but at a distance, and memorised them.

The next morning, John all ready with a camera, the pupils, excited about this 'extra-special' visit with a surprise in store for them, set off.

Leading them to the spot where he had first noticed the new, light grey gravestone, set on a patch of grass among the old ones, he hesitated, and suddenly stopped in his tracks. He knew they were at the exact spot where he had stood yesterday. Of course they were. There was the patch of green grass exactly as before – *but with no sign of the light, grey gravestone!* The pupils waited while John hurried over to where he had stood, remembering how something had told him 'not to move any closer'; but yes, no, his mind in a whirl, he had to accept the fact that there was nothing to be seen – nothing, nothing at all, except an empty patch of green grass.

• • •

Whereas with John, his experience in the old cemetery seemed unexplainable, Velda's was quite the opposite; in fact, it was 'predictable' – if you knew the history.

Velda lives on the Isle of Wight. She is a quiet, placid, happy lady with a good understanding of the other side (of life), and not usually phased out by any strange-seeming occurrences, that is, until...

On this particular summer's day, only a few years ago, Velda brought the washing in from the garden, and carefully laid a shirt out on the ironing board. Turning away for a moment, as she turned back and made ready to iron, she was startled to find the whole garment, the shirt, covered in green glitter! Green Glitter!! She was amazed, and quite 'thrown' by this state of affairs – there was no one else in the house at the time, and absolutely no glitter at all in the place. She stood transfixed in shock, as if in a stupor, staring at, of all things, an ordinary, humble ironing board, adorned with a shirt covered in green glitter.

It took a while, but gradually, as she stood there, so still and quiet, deep in thought, at first slowly, then in a sudden, huge burst of understanding, a smile lit up her face and she shouted out in pure joy, 'Doris! Doris!', the name of her close friend, now passed away. The predictable part of the tale was that Doris was mad about 'glitter', as everyone knew. Every possible item, gift, card, invitation, whatever, had to have a mass covering, or a sprinkle of glitter – no matter what time of year, no matter what the occasion (or even no occasion).

Marvelling at the sheer magic of it all, Velda, now with a mischievous smile beginning to curl at the corners of her mouth, while still weighing up the scene, stood there contentedly and happily. She contemplated memories of her dear friend and the wonder of how Doris had been determined and *able* to make a sure return, which, for Velda, there could be no doubt.

John had surveyed the old gravestone in the cemetery; he'd registered the whole scene so vividly in his mind, yet did not come to an understanding of what it was all about. Velda, meanwhile, had the answer to her experience almost immediately, as she witnessed what was to her, the obvious; her friend's determination to prove her survival of death in a way of which there could be no doubt – the materialisation of glitter.

There are marvels, wonders, miracles happening, every moment of every minute of life, somewhere; sometimes understandable, often unexplainable, but happening.

Emma: 'I was becoming more interested than ever in the paranormal, reading about it, studying it (in my own way), and wanting to talk about it at every opportunity with friends who were also interested. While out walking, I passed through a small market town just as a huge transporter carrying two tiers of new cars was passing through, heading towards me. It was dark blue, but not quite navy. Written in "gigantic" white letters above the cab and lying across the full width of the vehicle, was the word "SPIRIT". I stared in disbelief and turned to watch as it passed by, wondering if anyone else was as puzzled and amazed by the sight as I was, but of the few wandering around, no one else seemed to have noticed.'

A lady suffering with throat and mouth cancer coughed up the tumour, and a year later she was confirmed as cured. The doctor congratulated her!

Gina, two and a half years old, ran happily along the path, ahead of her family, on this her first visit to a cemetery, then suddenly stopped, and placed her hand on a gravestone. It was her grandfather's; the one they were visiting.

Questions, and sometimes answers, but what about the desperately sad question, most of us ask when, heart almost torn out with grief, facing overwhelmingly tragic circumstances, we call out, WHY?

Discussing this recently with a Catholic priest, I asked him if there was a verse or passage in the Bible that says we are not supposed to know certain things, not to look for reasons or answers to questions, such as the deeper meaning of life. 'It's not to say that we are not supposed to know,' was his considered reply, 'but we *can't* know. Our minds are not able to take in the mystery; mystery has layers and layers of meaning but we can't always comprehend, get to the bottom; we can try, but we have to have a sense of trust.'

• • •

A nature programme on TV, giving us an insight into the wonders and miracles of nature, explained how many of the problems we face in life 'have already been solved' by nature. But have you noticed that each time science makes a new discovery, after all the excitement and 'hype' have died down, it seems to be that the new discovery throws up yet more questions? Recently, in a European country, six scientists were in serious trouble for giving a wrong weather prediction!

A steadily growing band of scientists are coming round to the fact that there *is* more to life than we can see, or touch on materially or put in a test tube or whatever! There *are* people with special gifts for 'healing', 'seeing' (clairvoyance), and there are those who have proved that 'out of body', OBE experiences, 'near-death', ND, experiences, the gift of intuition, and many more gifts are for real! The 'aura', which is an energy field of the life force, emitting colours according to our state of health (well-being), surrounding a person or thing, has now been proved to exist. And with this proof from scientist Mitsuo Hiramtsu, it's official![3] Science is now proving that meditation and yoga can genetically change our bodies; that long-term practitioners of relaxation methods such as meditation and yoga have far more disease-fighting genes than those who do not practise any form of relaxation.

There has been, for some years, and steadily growing, a move towards scientists and theologians working together in small groups to try to present one unified vision of the world; in other words, to find the true meaning of interconnection. Lynne McTaggart, in her book, *The Field*, tells us:

'Far from destroying God, science for the first time was proving His existence – by demonstrating that a higher, collective consciousness was out there. There need no longer be two truths, the truth of science and the truth of religion. There could be one unified vision of the world.'

In her prologue to the book, McTaggart explains that, 'At the very frontier of science discoveries are being made that prove what religion has always espoused; that human beings are far more extraordinary than an assemblage of flesh and bones.'[4]

Thinking back to the section, earlier in the chapter, on the 'Aquarian Age', our age, the time in which we are now living, it was forecast in past centuries to be the age of a spiritual revolution; in other words, the time for humanity to return to its spiritual roots. Along with the 'scorn' meted out to this seemingly incredulous idea, is the question, 'How can this be?' A 'spiritual' age! A 'more spiritual' age? And alongside the apparent impossibility of this 'spiritual age' being almost upon us, despite the dreadful state of everything, worldwide, chinks of light (pointing towards our salvation) are turning, slowly but surely, into shafts of light and moving towards 'beacons', as we begin to turn the ship, so to speak, at last, in the right direction.

The growing number of people interested in books on spiritual matters, including the paranormal, holistic healing, books on alternate remedies, yoga, meditation, and so on is remarkable. One editor has observed that the public awareness of the fact that we are more than just our physical bodies is perhaps greater today than at any time in our history, and the numbers attending psychic fairs, and who are seeking spiritual healing, is greater than ever.

(There is a rising tide of consciousness leading to a flood of understanding, an awakening; a spiritual awakening in our time.)

The Angel phenomenon has really 'taken off' in recent years, with people often accepting (small?) evidence of angel intervention; stories of angelic presence and so on, seeming to be almost an everyday occurrence, and accepted as such. (Finding a feather on the path directly in front of you or on your doorstep is recognised as a sign.)

In *A Letter from Oslo*,[5] we read that Princess Martha Louise, who is fourth in line to the throne in Norway's royal family, 'talks to angels'. She believes angels look over us and appear as auras around our bodies. Princess Louise has opened a therapy centre, with courses in spiritual healing, and she teaches students to get in touch with the 'divine universe'.

In 2012 one Sunday morning, thousands of residents were left in awe when they saw a beautiful angel-shaped cloud drifting above their homes. It was so large people could see it over thirty miles away. Electrician Michael Robinson spotted it as he looked out of his bedroom window. He reported being 'stunned', to say the least, to see this incredible 'angel-shaped cloud hovering in the sky'. Retired lecturer Michael Mitchel also saw the 'angel' from his home in Derby and didn't know what it was but thought it was an 'apparition from beyond'.

A perfectly shaped angel cloud stunned New Yorkers as it hovered over the city in 1995. There were countless pictures taken and the event recorded in at least one book.

Does it not give us 'pause for thought' that, now, in our time, in this (one hundred percent?) science-focused, materialistic age, we can look for, and accept, the presence of angels. Angels feature in probably all religions, there are at least three hundred references to them in the Bible, and, just as there is a return to the choice of a biblical name for a new baby – or whoever – could this be simply 'fashion'? Or could there be something more behind it as we have been informed (and here we are back to another of the prophecies relating to the age of Aquarius) 'children of this age and newly born into this age, will be born with special spiritual gifts and understanding'.

Little Anne is just over two years old and has, for some time, been recognised to be 'psychic'. She plays with spirit children and she has been 'heard' saying to them, after playing a while, 'Oh you can go home now.' She is way ahead of other children who are the same age, and this has been 'noticed' and commented on by not only those at the nursery she attends. Anne comes out with things others would not even know about. Recently, while playing in the park – she was there with her parents – she pointed to a man who was walking across the grass, and said, 'Ghost.' Her dad, turning white, saw the same man. He was a friend of theirs who had died a few months previously.

Think about how even the majority of us now perhaps accept 'experiences' related to us (or our own experiences) easily; and how readily we listen to such tales, putting in the odd word or two, 'marvellous', 'incredible', 'really!', and mean it! Even the doubters who remark, 'Well, I don't believe in anything,' usually have to add the word, 'But…', then they go on to quote something that happened in their own lives, that they could never quite understand, and still puzzle over, years later. We know, however, that it is not so long ago when things of the so-called paranormal 'were not discussed' as openly or freely as they are today; and certainly not accepted as a natural part of life as they are today. Our acceptance of, in such a big way, the 'angel' phenomena we have just considered is proof enough of that.

Angels appear in the Bible from beginning to end, from the book of Genesis to the book of Revelation, and as we have just noted, there are at least 300 references to them. As spirit messengers, angels are sent to help us in all our ways on the road through life; comforting, encouraging, advising, and often giving us messages while we sleep.[6]

We are urged to take notice, pay attention to our dreams, but if there *is* an angel message there for us and we misunderstand, or forget it, we are assured, in the scriptures, that angels will return and repeat messages until we do understand them, until we *do* 'get the message', so to speak.[7]

You have your own guardian angel, as do 'I and each and every one of us'; our angel guide to turn to and help us in time of need,[8] but at some point in your life (maybe often), you must have suddenly, for no apparent reason, felt a surge of confidence, trust, happiness, a certainty that 'yes', all is well. When this happens, you can know that your guardian angel is very close.[9]

Angels often appear in human form.[10]

How many times have we perhaps met one and did not realise...?[11]

We can only ask (although we are told in the Bible) 'How did the people, the ordinary 'citizens' of the time, react to the spectacular events – escapes, healings, mysteries – happening around them, events not only concerning angels?

In the story of the conversion of Saul on the road to Damascus, we learn that,

'Men stood speechless, hearing a

Voice but seeing no man'.[12]

(An experience we would probably be quite comfortable with, today.)

The parting of the Red Sea is one of the most dramatic episodes in the Old Testament, when Moses and the Israelites are trapped between Pharaoh's advancing chariots and a wall of water. Thanks to 'divine intervention', a mighty east wind blows all night, splitting the waters to leave a passage of dry land with walls of water on both sides. The Israelites then make their escape.

New research has shown that this could well have happened

with freak weather conditions – a powerful wind could have divided the waters just as depicted in the Bible.[13]

Zacchaeus, the tax collector, was a short man who was determined to see Jesus, the wonderful preacher and healer he had heard so much about. Zacchaeus also knew he would never see him in all the crowds also waiting to see Jesus, and so he had a good idea; he would climb a tree, a sycamore tree, and this he did. Jesus in passing, looked up and saw him – being a tax collector, he was not popular with the crowds (not even in those days). Then, when Jesus called up to Zacchaeus, 'Come down,' and told him he wanted to visit his house, although Zacchaeus was overjoyed at this, the crowds were not pleased – just as they probably wouldn't be today. [14]

During the persecution of the Christians, after the death of Jesus – James the apostle had been killed – people were fearful for the safety of Peter who had been arrested; and we know that they (the Christians) prayed fervently and unceasingly for his release.

Meanwhile, Peter sat in his prison cell, chained, between two soldiers, with two prison guards positioned on duty outside the main gates. Peter and the soldiers were sound asleep when a bright light flooded the cell and an angel appeared. The angel shook Peter to wake him, telling him to get up quickly, which he did, and as he stood up, his chains fell off (Peter thinking this was all a vision). The angel then told him to throw his cloak around himself, 'and follow me', Peter still believing it was a vision.

They passed through gates that opened of their own accord, the angel leading Peter safely into the city and to a labyrinth of streets where he left him; Peter soon made his way to a 'safe' house, where he knew he would find his friends, the Christians, gathered.

There are such exciting, miraculous stories from the Bible, many involving angels, and so many unbelievable, diverse experiences happening now, in our own time, and that have happened throughout history, since the beginning of time – experiences that are, apart from being passed around from 'mouth to mouth', not usually reported on. Only a few make the headlines. Many historians, philosophers, 'thinkers' would agree that there *are* ancient myths, legends, folklore, that are based on truth; remember the old saying 'fact is stranger than fiction'.

An expert on the reactions that affect people who have 'falls from high places', worked with survivors of the 9/11 disaster in America, on anything and everything to do with incident. One survivor telling of the horror of being trapped in the tower block and, finally, not being able to stand it anymore, thought of 'ending it all', until a voice said, 'Don't give up', and he didn't. The expert, who has through his work, amassed a huge collated data of facts and information, made the following statement:

> 'For anyone who survives above a fifth floor, it's grim.
> They must have the wings of angels.'

The following is an account, witnessed by many people, of a fall from a balcony under construction on a building site in Johannesburg, South Africa, in 1972, from the seventh floor, eighty feet up.

'Working on the balcony, Peter stepped back, lost his footing, and fell through scaffolding into the ditch below. Miraculously, he got up and started to walk away. One of his men, who had been working at ground level, picked up his glasses which had shot off during the impact of the fall, handed them to him saying, 'Here boss'.

The site foreman, and other workers who were in the site cabin at the time, saw him fall, and stunned, froze on the spot. No one wanted to go and see what was left of his body lying in the ditch. They were even more stunned when his head appeared over the side as, scrambling up the side of the ditch, he made his way towards them. After countless x-rays at two hospitals, he was found to have only one small rib bone broken in his back.

His wife arrived at the site a few hours later to collect his car. The site foreman met her. He was obviously still in a state of shock as he told her that, although they did not believe in such things, both he and the other workmen who had witnessed the accident had come to the same conclusion. 'Your husband was caught and held by invisible arms.'[15]

There are and always have been miracles, floods, earthquakes, fires, all happening worldwide and on an unimaginable scale, often heralding a time of serious change that leads in turn to a forced re-thinking of 'the way we live'. Miracles, floods, earthquakes, fires, riots, and people power is on the rise too. Ordinary citizens, tired of injustices, of being downtrodden, sick of dominating, power-mad autocrats, are determined to make a difference in forging a better way of life for everyone; determined, dedicated to making a difference, and the difference is happening *now*. We are witnessing the unravelling of the establishment (the way it has been); a demand for a new transparency, for accountability, for fairness in government and in all transactions, worldwide or local, community-based, however humble. There is a new demand for sharing, caring; protection for our world and *all* its citizens/ members – and here we include (we are gradually learning to include) the natural world and of course, the animal kingdom.

'If there's no home for nature, there will be no nature. Give nature a home.'[16]

There is a new, strong realisation – particularly among the young of today, that the answers to our troubled world will not be found in lives focused solely on money. Money, material success, possessions, power, 'greed'; for out of all the chaos, the turmoil, the unspeakable atrocities, unbridled violence, the wrecking, wrecking, wrecking, we hear about day after day, there is a stirring among society worldwide; a whispering… 'No!' There is a universal shout, 'Enough is Enough!' It is time for change; *time for change*, and the way we must go, the path we must take, 'is being pointed out to us in no uncertain terms', for just as great advances have been made in technology, in science, and are being made every day, so too there is:

'A rising tide of consciousness leading to a flood of understanding, an awakening, a spiritual awakening in our time.'

A quietly strong revolution is taking place in our world today. Across oceans and deserts and cities and towns and villages, tiny hamlets and solitary places, high mountain ranges and green prairies, cold regions and hot ones, everywhere, dramatic changes of near gigantic proportion are taking place; dramatic changes that are heralding in the 'new age', the age of Aquarius.

The new age, in which it is said that humanity will be forced to move onto a higher consciousness, 'awareness', will change our way of living to a more spiritual, less materialistic, selfish society.

Remember the story of the people of Atlantis who were so clever, so technologically advanced, with wealth beyond measure, living in a futuristic, high luxury society, and so completely absorbed with power and greed and selfishness that they forgot their 'true selves'. During the course of one day and night their home, the island of Atlantis, was 'swallowed up by the sea' and vanished.

We cannot avoid the changes that are happening in our world today, but we can be part of the crusade to see that the 'changes', and what happens in the aftermath of the changes, will be for the better.[17]

The advanced 'technology' we are now part of is moving hand in hand with a new thinking, an attempt, to link into and encourage, the emotional/intellectual/creative (spiritual), side of our nature, through the arts... . We are living in a time of surreal, live, creativity, with a 'hands on' approach that is quite revolutionary.

Can you imagine walking into an empty art gallery; standing, staring, walking around lost, wondering what on earth is going on? (Provocative and thoughtful, suggesting the absence of something, making you *think* about what or who was present.)

There are art galleries where you find rooms with empty walls, some with blank pieces of paper and empty canvases, with only the name of the painting and artist displayed. (All about firing the imagination…) Actors might be 'employed' as visitors to encourage the 'real' visitors to 'think about what they are not seeing!' and to visualise, to stir up their own ideas. There might be an empty room with only a few tiny notices dotted around here and there, again, for visitors to stand and think and really ponder on what it is all about; and there could be another room, with invisible space, where you walk around with headphones on, that make a sound when you hit an invisible wall. Yes, there will be many who disagree with these ideas, write them off as 'crazy', but, to look at it another way, even the disagreement will be fruitful if it encourages dialogue…

A 'thought' garden was featured at this year's Chelsea Flower Show; and have you noticed that more and more programmes on both radio and television are encouraging us to 'think' about the programme and respond with our own views or opinions. There is a move, an innovation, to add suitable music while viewing real paintings – this an attempt to link the arts, giving yet more drive, urge, to encourage feelings, impressions; perception through the senses – warmth, pain, longing.

A growing number of schools are putting 'meditation' time on their programme, even for very young children who need to learn to have 'quiet time', and to learn not to 'shout' so much… a big and growing concern among youngsters who don't seem to be able to simply 'talk'!

How about going to the theatre and finding yourself part of the play, the action, along with the cast? That's audience participation in the full, with actors sometimes given only the plot and a brief story line to follow.

'Flash Mob', is a form of performing art that has brought a lot of fun into sometimes drab, dreary lives, when, quietly going about your own affairs – it could be anywhere there is a crowd of people, at a railway station, a busy market, in the mall, walking around the shops, when, suddenly, music blares out. Then it could be one or two ordinary-looking people (by ordinary I mean not in fancy dress or costume of any kind), start dancing, just 'out of the blue'. At first, staring in disbelief, you might (hopefully), and as they encourage you (and before you know where you are), start to join in. You and those around you, picking up the beat so to speak, let yourselves go, have the time of your life.

Outward events impinging on our lives in little bursts of energy that make us sit up and take notice, or get moving and dance! Outbursts of individuality that (unknowingly advancing the prophecy of this age) can take us to a different level of existence, touching on a depth of feeling and understanding that transcends the mere mundane, everyday existence, finding us perhaps, responding as never before, to the higher side of life, and in so doing, giving prominence to the spiritual.

The Arts, in some strange, mysterious way, bring the spiritual side of our nature, the real you, the real me, forward, and take their rightful place, as a natural part of our everyday lives.

This is the age of prophesies being fulfilled; and so we come to the prophesy, the promise of a saviour, a messiah, an avatar, a teacher who will return to the earth plane to help us, guide us through the hard times we are living in. Talked about for centuries, it could happen in this our 'now time', but if this is so, where will it happen? Is the promise already being 'fulfilled', or is it in the process of being 'fulfilled'? How, when, where, who, or what? Perhaps you already have your own ideas, certainties even, about this; or is there a 'something else' in the equation for us to 'really' understand the promise of this teacher to come? Is there something we have missed, overlooked, in the understanding of the prophesy? Something we have misunderstood...? Because happen it will, of this there is no doubt. It *has* to happen...to save us, and soon.

• • •

Standing in a queue behind a group of 'with it', 'cool', as they say, teenagers, having a bit of fun, a good laugh amongst themselves, I noticed that one of them, maybe about eighteen years old, had a striking tattoo on the calf of her leg. It was large, colourful, and particularly impressive, depicting two wings and a heart entwined with the words 'All my hope is in God'.[18] A lady, standing beside me in the queue, also noticed it, and couldn't resist asking, 'Do you believe that?' To which the teenager, turning to face us, gave a prompt and positive reply: 'Oh yes!' and at that, turned back to continue her chat, and a good laugh with her friends.

Flash, Bang, Wallop, Hold! What a photograph! Grandpa, straight back, seated, baby on his lap. Grandma close behind him, family grouped around, all posing for the picture...

Chapter Two

We are Two Worlds. We are spiritual beings in a physical body living in a material world.

'For now we see through a glass darkly', Cor 1 – 13-12

WITH AMAZING STORIES TO read (and weighty evidence), giving proof of the reality of the spirit world, we can gain a little more understanding of the difference between ghosts and real spirit people, and energies. Also by being made aware of the tremendous effort and energy and planning needed – behind the scenes – for the spirit world to produce any evidence at all, this chapter hopes to bring the awareness, even the certainty, in more ways than one, that we are, you and me, indeed two worlds.

We stood talking in a car park as it was getting dark. It was a bitterly cold winter's night but Ann wanted to talk and probably didn't even feel the cold, or the light wind making the air seem even colder as it wrapped in and around us; while I, quietly, unobtrusively, tried to manoeuvre for a little shelter between cars. In the light of a street lamp, I noticed tears welling in Anne's eyes, and not from the cold. She struggled to find the right words, as befitting what she wanted to say. There was no doubting the sincerity in her voice. Quiet and deep thinking, Ann had a tale to tell; a tale she would only trust with someone she knew would respect and understand her story. I felt privileged to know that, this time anyway, that person was me.

Years ago, one bright, warm, summer morning, Ann enjoyed the pleasant feeling of waking up thoroughly refreshed after a good night's sleep. Stretching, yawning, and slowly bringing her-self up to a sitting position, still in bed, eyes wide open and already fully awake, she was given, what she felt was a startling, amazing, larger than life 'wake-up call'. It was a sight Ann still feels incredible to believe, but which she knows is true, down to the last detail. Here is the experience she related, *relived,* to me, in the car park, that night; and in spite of the cold, and the wind, and the dark, and the 'wanting to get home quickly feeling' (well, I did), as she wistfully told her tale, no one was in a hurry to leave.

Ann had the best seat in the house, she had a 'ringside' seat, as she sat there, comfortably in her bed, fully awake, a captive audience for the show of a 'lifetime'; a scene played out before her as if from some Victorian melodrama, the whole thing spontaneous, vivid, surreal...

Her whole family, now passed over on the other side of life, 'dead', as some would say, were 'assembled' together, posing, as though making ready to have a family photograph taken. Ann had, for a long time, without ever 'delving' into such things, or even being particularly interested, experienced so-called phenomena from the spirit world. She 'naturally' heard and saw; it might be a fleeting glimpse of a figure; a voice calling her name from another room when she knew no one was there; a 'premonition', a feeling, but this was different. This was so different that it was almost as if all the other experiences had been preparing her, leading up to this very special moment; and it was a special moment, with a 'message'.

There were her grandparents, aunts and uncles, cousins, the younger family members grouped around the sides and sitting 'cross legged' on the floor at the front, all posing for the picture… . Her grandmother stood behind her grandfather, hand resting on his shoulder, but 'centrepiece' was taken by her grandfather, who tenderly cushioned in his arms, and held out, as if to her (to Ann), a newborn baby. It was her baby; the one she had worried over and pined over since the loss, and still – and in spite of having following family – missed and loved.

Tears could not blur the vision, nor sadness lessen her gentle smile, as she played 'audience' to this outstanding display of evidence from the other side of life, on that morning, so long ago. It was evidence of a family united and determined to show her the baby she so badly grieved over, thought lost, but now found. Found, and there, with her, in that very room, being portrayed as the star of the show, but a show with a message, a message of hope and comfort from the world of spirit.

It was, at first, in pure astonishment, then with humble gratitude, that Ann finally grasped the true meaning behind it all. The experience was 'devised', well thought out, and enacted, in such a clever way by spirit, to give her 'evidence', her own proof, not only of the survival of her little one, but that the baby was safe and well, being cared for, and the centre of a loving family… her family; her own family.

• • •

Are you the sort of person who is curious about the backstage activity, as you enjoy some performance or other? Can you believe that there is often hard, physical work, with intense concentration and co-operation needed between all backstage hands, to get everything 'just right', to make the difference between first-class and mediocre performances. There are so many considerations to take into account on both sides of the curtain, with necessary rules and regulations to adhere to. (For instance, a talented young magician, in the middle of a successful summer season, was sacked because someone, side-stage, had touched, tampered with, perhaps accidently, a piece of equipment set up ready to be moved front stage at a certain point in his act – he failed!)

Behind the scenes, focusing on sustained effort, along with trained, professional organisation and skill, in any theatrical production or performance, and so it is with any contact evidence and phenomena relayed between our two worlds. For starters, the recipient of the message (evidence) has to be at the right place at the right time, for the huge amount of energy required to produce the 'evidence' to be relevant. For every seemingly tiny piece of evidence, planning and precision is vital; a 'flick of the hair' while quietly reading and no one else around; a tap on the shoulder we know is not imagined, again, no one else there. A sudden whiff of unusual perfume; a shadow glimpsed out of the corner of the eye; an unexpected meeting with someone from out of the past who we know, had to be 'more than coincidence'. Messages, evidence, however short or seemingly insignificant – by the way – no true contact from the other side of life is ever insignificant, but a blessing to receive; *devised, well thought out and enacted in such a clever way, by spirit, to give evidence of survival.*

Edith, well used to seeing and hearing spirit since a young girl, was delighted to see, as she passed through her living room, a big-built lady, probably middle-aged, no coat on, standing pushed into the corner of the room, behind the television set – knitting. She didn't look up at all, take any notice, of Edith's presence, but simply stood there, intent on her work. Poor Edith, her first thought was that she did not like the idea of this 'lady', this 'big' lady, being squashed in the corner behind the television set; so what was it all about? Perhaps she just wanted to say hello, which she didn't, much to Edith's disappointment; but obviously, the lady took her own presence there for granted, not being at all concerned about being crammed in a corner behind a TV in Edith's living room. Perhaps this room had been *her* area, anyway, a long time ago; it might even have been her home.

Here, with Edith's knowledge and understanding, having witnessed many types of phenomena, she realises that we could be talking about her having seen a 'ghost', not a real spirit person. There is a belief that a 'ghost' is a 'replay of a memory', or an image from the past.

A good example that points out the difference between ghosts and the real 'spirit world' is the story of two families with four young children sharing a big house in Spain as a holiday home. The house had an old part and a new part, the new part housing a playroom, ideal for their children. The holiday was a great success, and the parents quizzed the children at the airport on the way home, as to why they did not seem to use the playroom: they were shocked at the reply, 'Because it was full with the other children, they didn't want us.'

Hearing these words, and knowing there were no other children in the house, and also knowing that their little ones could not have invented such a story, the whole atmosphere of carefree happiness immediately changed for the grown-ups, as they froze on the spot, at the significance of what they had just heard.

Later, at home, when Geoff questioned his young daughter about the 'other children', he turned icy cold at her reply: 'A little Spanish girl often came and sat on my bed talking to me.'[1]

Returning to the theme of ghosts as a memory, or an image from the past, it is interesting to note that the playroom was in the new part of the house, therefore making it more likely that the evidence pointed to the children having indeed witnessed 'real' spirit children.

Moving on to Kevin's experience, we seem to be again in

touch with the spirit world, where a well-planned effort, a clever 'working behind the scenes' was engineered, so that everything was in place and ready to give a message of reassurance, so badly needed at the time.

Kevin, a successful and popular hair stylist, grieved for his mother whom he had always been close to, and cared for, until her passing some four years ago. He had experienced evidence twice of her continued existence. The first one, feeling a hand on his shoulder as he struggled with a bit of gardening 'to keep the place tidy'; the second one, something to do with a watch, but then came an experience, to Kevin, so positive and convincing that, uplifted, comforted and happy, he was at last able to get on with his life.

For a long time, Kevin had enjoyed weekends away in London. Sometimes alone, sometimes with friends, but now, since his mother's death, he did not look forward to these weekends at all; with no real interest or enthusiasm, for him, they were just weekends away with somewhere to go, something to do.

At the start of this particular weekend (in London), he arrived at the hotel, checked in, found his room, all as usual. He visited the bathroom, and felt drawn to notice the bath towel, that seemed to be set in a peculiar way, 'turned over', or was it a corner 'turned over', revealing the label? A label that, on seeing it, with its bold, strong, lettering, made him 'numb' with shock; his eyes filled with tears, as it silently portrayed to him the name 'Isabella'. Isabella was his mother's name.

It took a while for Kevin to accept the reality of this piece of evidence, the enormity of its meaning, the love it brought him. However, after the initial shock, came the comfort; and it came in a great swell of relief, as the heavy burden of sorrow he had carried, lifted, evaporated, disappeared, became as mist on the wall. Kevin had a fantastic weekend, taking the first, serious steps, to rebuilding his otherwise shattered life.

Have *you* ever had a so-called paranormal experience? That special moment, when you know you have touched on something that, leaving its mark, you will never forget. It could have been a dream, a life-moment triviality; a sad, serious, or happy, uplifting experience; a telephone call, an unexpected meeting, an 'out of the blue', sudden change in your life that had startling repercussions. When people have a paranormal experience, they know they have had one, and no one can convince them otherwise.

Have you ever sat back in a deep, thoughtful mood, and asked yourself, 'What is it all about?' (Life) Expressing this heart-felt desire for understanding the true meaning of why we are here, and all that, is probably the biggest of any question we will ever ask, and involves, perhaps just for a fleeting moment, us touching on 'the divine within'.

'Seek and ye shall find,' we are advised in the Bible.[2]

Our spirit self, which is our true self, wants us, urges us, to look a little more closely at life; to see things for what they really are, and not as, perhaps, superficially portrayed. President Obama, in his book *The Audacity of Hope*, writes moving words on people needing to know that there is something more to life than the daily round, the common task; 'they (Americans) are deciding that their work, their possessions, their diversions, their sheer busyness are not enough. They need an assurance that somebody out there does care about them, is listening to them – that they are not just destined to travel down a long highway towards nothingness.'[3]

Life, with all its twists and turns, can appear both beautiful and ugly, anything and everything, yet sometimes feel as nothing. It can seem a game, often likened to a paper chase where we hunt for clues, and in a sort of 'reverie' maybe wonder, among other things, about fate; is there such a thing, and what makes the wise so wise, the rich so rich, the poor so poor? And on it goes.

Then there is the conundrum, the mischievousness, the

illusiveness, of time, which is in itself fickle, and, as we are told, non-existent in the spirit world.

Time: where in one circumstance, a single hour can seem like an eternity when we are anxious for news, or in a worrying, distressing, situation, not pass over quickly enough. Yet in those wondrous, captivating moments we try to hold onto (hopefully we have all experienced them) time flies past as nothing.

John, now a senior citizen, remembers his strange feelings on re-visiting an old church in the bush-land of South Africa. He used to visit the church as a young seaman, when he was in the merchant navy. He recalls always sitting in the same pew, enjoying the solitude, the silence. Recalling his feelings when he returned decades later, as he again sat in the same pew, in the solitude and silence, he was amazed to find that nothing had changed; all was as before, and was as in the memories he had vividly kept in his mind, always hoping to return. The strangeness he felt, on his return visit, and with such overwhelming emotion, was in the attack he experienced of 'as if it were yesterday', syndrome; the distant past (all else seemingly erased) suddenly hitting him as the reality...

Going back somewhere, after a lifetime away, can engender 'disbelief', even if only for a moment, in all that has happened since. To sit in exactly the same place, finding everything is as it was decades ago, can be quite chilling, causing you to believe that 'time' itself is unreal – is it? – and does not, in fact, exist at all. Everything you have experienced, cherished, witnessed, all you have achieved in life since those earlier, faraway days of being 'there' (at that certain place) appear to disappear as you go *back, back, back*; the reliving of memories now brought to the forefront of your mind, blurring all the 'in between'.

It is remarkable to think that time, non-existent in the spirit world, plays such a major part of life here on earth and yet, from evidence, it appears to be that it is not too difficult an adjustment to make on the other side.

Bricks in walls look out unblinkingly at human effort and have seen it all, know it all; and time worn pavements, bearing the imprint of long gone footsteps, 'know'.

It is 'time' itself that stuns; it is time that leaves its mark on the human frame and mind, and yet can seem as nothing when, with the blink of some memory from another time, another place… it is all gone, all finished.

Time, just an imprint of a 'recalling'. The 'echo' of a memory of what we were; of what was. Yet it can make us what we are?

• • •

'Time' does not exist in the spirit world, but could 'time' be a factor in understanding the following experiences that happened to Eva and Derek over thirty years ago?

There were a number of confrontational issues for Eva and Derek to think about that Christmas of 1979. Financial worries, including the sudden absconding of a business partner (a small business) to Australia, with Derek left to pay the bills, and face the music, so to speak. Having recently moved into a newly built house with all the stresses and strains associated with a move, especially to a new property, things were not easy.

Late on this particular night, they had just returned from visiting friends who lived over thirty miles away in the next county, Eva was driving. Arriving home, she pulled onto the driveway, stopped the car, got out, and as she did so, noticed a black hole inside the gold coin ring she wore on her right forefinger. Startled to see this, she then realised that the gold coin was missing. Derek, after scrambling around looking for it on the drivers' side of the car, soon found it, but they were both aware of how easily it could have been lost altogether, if the same thing had happened somewhere else, away from home. As pleased as they were to have found it, there was something about the whole incident that made them think 'how strange'.

Days later, the jeweller was also 'surprised' by their story, saying how unlikely it was for such a thing to happen, especially with a new ring, and he was even more puzzled as, easily and securely, he 'clicked' the coin back into place.

Christmas over, *and* New Year celebrations, it was time to take down the tree that stood proudly in the large bow window of the house; a tree packed with toys and lights, baubles, tiny gift boxes, cards, sparkly streamers, tinsel, the lot! Eva, not having seen it lit up in all its glory from outside, decided, just before it was time to dismantle it, to walk across the space opposite (planned by the builders to be made into a small, landscaped garden) onto a path by the road, and view it from there.

Wrapping up well, as it was a bitterly cold night, and leaving Derek in the house, she made her way to the path by the road, where she stood immediately opposite the house, with a full, good view of the tree. Yes, she was 'more than pleased'. It looked splendid, and after a few more minutes of 'admiring', made to turn and leave...but then, what happened?

As she made to turn, 'astonished, amazed, then dismayed', all at once, she saw the tree, her beautiful Christmas tree, with all its toys and baubles and cards – suddenly sway from side to side right across the window and back, three or four times, in full, big, wide, sweeps, almost as if it was waving to her. Shocked, then devastated, unbelieving that Derek could do such a thing; he was always so careful and gentle, this was completely 'out of character' for him, how could he?

Slowly making her way back to the house, all she could think of was the 'unholy' mess to clear up, with toys, lights, cards, tinsel, and all the tree needles sticking to everything, everywhere. 'What a mess!' The words kept going round and round in her head. How, why? You couldn't make it up; and they had her parents and a friend due to call at any moment. Her thoughts in turmoil, and now in an angry mood, Eva made her way home, determined to 'scream' at Derek and not half give him a piece of her mind. How could he?

Derek opened the door, giving yet another shock to Eva as she saw his face, whiter than white, almost 'shining' in the darkness of the hall; a mask, his stance seemingly bowed and, 'was he shaking'? 'What on earth?' were the only words she could utter as, quietened by his strange appearance, she followed him into the living room. There she found the Christmas tree, standing tall and upright, as before, in all its glory, with not a branch out of place; not a toy, not a card fallen; not a bauble disturbed, not a hint of mess with pine needles piled up and lying all over the floor. Eva and Derek stood in silence, staring at the tree, then at each other. The moment was only broken when Derek, perhaps even more in shock than Eva, carefully explained, how he was sitting quietly on the sofa, when the tree suddenly 'took off', lurching from side to side in a big way, about three or four times (exactly as seen by Eva). Then he experienced the shock of finding nothing had been disturbed, nothing had been put out of place in the process; all was exactly as before, as if nothing had happened, but he knew that it had, and, for confirmation for each other, so did Eva.

Later, Eva said about the incident, 'All I know is – it happened. I don't know how, or why, but, having an interest, and a little knowledge about such things [the paranormal], on thinking it over, I did wonder if it was a "message". Then, linking it up with the coin falling out of the ring only a few days earlier, but not losing it, I wondered, could it be the same with the tree? Nothing spoilt, all's well in the end.'

Likening the incidents to their lives at the time (and for some years into the future), when, through no fault of their own, they stood to lose everything they already had, and had worked hard for, they did wonder if they had been given a message of 'hope'. 'Don't give up when the real rough times come,' and come they did, 'fast and furious'; but they didn't give up. Instead, they stood 'tall' together, like the Christmas tree; and after a long time of constant worry and heartache, came into their own with more than they had ever dared hope for, and of course, the best thing of all, they had each other, and their special 'message', which eventually they knew had to be from the spirit world.

Just as an after-thought regarding the above two experiences here recorded; messages from the Bible were often given in parables, stories told to illustrate a spiritual truth, sometimes told as a riddle.

• • •

Understanding that we, 'us humans', are vibrating energy – more about this over the page – with our own personal vibration, and thinking along these lines in this, our modern, hi-tech world, in trying to understand the thinking behind, say, mobile phones, could we possibly be moving a little closer to believing in, and even to having a little understanding, of 'spirit'?

With the amazing and startling advances in new technology, and something 'newer' out every day, are we, as 'lay' people, of course, perhaps beginning to understand the thinking 'behind' electronics. Energy, vibrations, rays, speed of light, sound, frequency and so on; perhaps we are *beginning* and even 'encouraged' to move a little closer towards understanding the possibility, and for many of us, the reality of a world of spirit.

Impinging as it does on our world, the spirit world is not 'found' above us (as a heaven in the sky), nor below, nor anywhere but here and now, mingling in with our own material world. 'Closer than hands and feet' is an old expression of believers – mingling in with our own material world, while struggling to lower the high vibrations of spirit to the dense, heavy, material atmosphere of the earth plane.

Perhaps one of the easiest ways to think about our two worlds is to liken them to a child's spinning top. When the top is stationery – as is in our world – we can see all the brilliant colours and patterns; however, when the top is in motion, wrapped up in fast spinning, they are lost, and the colours and patterns gone from our sight. They have moved as a result of the spinning on to a far higher vibration and are not visible to our ordinary, mortal eyes.

Mediums, seers, people who have the gift of 'second sight', can 'tune in'. They have learnt the art of lifting their own – our own – dense, heavy, material (earth) vibrations, on to the higher plane. Again, it is all about 'tuning in' to a higher frequency.

This new age, the Age of Aquarius, forecasts that humanity will be forced to move onto a higher 'vibration', 'consciousness', 'awareness', therefore changing our way of living to a more spiritual, less materialistic, less selfish society.

The spirit people, those who have passed on to the other side of life, the citizens of heaven, wanting to communicate, learn to help the procedure by lowering their own vibrations (apparently not easy), to link in, to tune in, make contact. The same principle seems to apply to healing, and to any other form of communication that seeks to unite the 'two worlds'.[4]

Penney Peirce, in her book *Frequency* writes, 'Everything is vibrating energy, and each of us has a personal vibration – a frequency of energy held moment by moment in our spirit, thoughts, emotions, and body – that communicates who we are to the world and helps shape our reality.'[5]

As part of the forecast for the 'age' we are now living in, the Age of Aquarius, it has been prophesied that we will move to being a more spiritual society, therefore caring about each other and *all* creation, as we raise our vibrations, consciousness, awareness, to the realisation that there *is* more to life than what we can see, or feel, or touch. It appears to be that we also move from the Information Age to the Age of Intuition. In line with the current trend, there is an increasing take-up of Spiritual Healing, Reiki, Reflexology, and other alternate therapies: taking up yoga, meditation; looking 'openly', not afraid to speak out about the other side of life; encompassing 'angels', guides, helpers; interpreting, looking for the meaning behind dreams; signs, symbols; lighting candles, often with small, private ceremonies to mark an anniversary, or perhaps a 'passing'.

The Age of Intuition is where we begin to rely on and understand the reality of our 'intuitive energy', a faculty we all possess, but one that has lain dormant in human kind for far too long. It has lain dormant in humans, but not, however, in animals…or birds…

• • •

At the Battle of Passchendaele, in October 1917, locked in combat in the mud of the battle, British troops needed to get an urgent signal back to their headquarters from the front line.

A messenger was despatched on a journey that should have taken twenty minutes, but, shortly after setting off, the courier came under fire. A bullet broke a leg and passed out of the body through the back, while the small metal message cylinder remained 'embedded' in the side.

Despite these horrendous injuries, the messenger dutifully continued, finally completing the mission, delivering the message after an agonising journey of over twenty-one hours – before dying the next day.

This feat of endurance, and perseverance, was achieved, not by a soldier, but by a pigeon, known only as 2709; one of thousands to serve – and die – in the First World War.

It has been proved that all life (plants do respond to love and TLC), all creatures, possess feelings, including a psychic awareness, along with the commendable attributes of loyalty and devotion.

During an offensive in October 1918, a pigeon, released at a front line post, carried a message for headquarters at Rampont, twenty-five miles away.

The enemy had laid down a bombardment prior to an attack and the bird had to fly through the fire, gaining altitude before he could get his bearings. The men below watched as a shell exploded close to him, the concussion sending him down. However, he regained his height and was able to continue, arriving at Rampont, twenty-five minutes later.

A bullet had ripped his breast, while bits of shrapnel had torn his body and his right leg was missing. The message tube, intact, was hanging by the ligaments of the torn leg.

He was nursed back to health, dying in 1935, at the age of seventeen.

'Honoured: the WW1 pigeons who earned their wings.'

A new exhibition highlights the contribution made by messenger pigeons in both world wars, when they were 'credited' with saving thousands of lives, and altering the course of battles. More than 100,000 served with British forces in the First World War, with a success ratio of 95 per cent in getting their messages through.

In 1943 the Dickin Medal was instituted to honour the contributions of all animals in conflict.[6]

It's a further reminder to us that we are all part of the great, big, amazing, miraculous universe, every living thing; and that, in the story of life, we need each other.

We lift our vibrations, moving on to being a more spiritual society, where we care about each other, and *all* life, *all* creation, as we come to realise, at last, that we don't own the planet…

In our world, where everything is vibrating, with waves of energy travelling in every direction everywhere, have you ever stopped and thought about the fact – the fact that countless invisible waves and vibrations are unceasingly circling, moving, around us; weaving, crisscrossing, on-going…?

Have you ever stood and gazed, in awe, at the night sky? Have you quietly taken in all its beauty and perfection as it displays, for us, 'the harmony of the heavens'. Albert Camus, author, explains that the world is never quiet, even its silence eternally resounds with the same notes, in vibrations that escape our ears, and Donald Hatch Andrews talks about the universe being 'more like music than matter'.

Have you ever heard the music of the spheres, the stars 'singing'? Hazel tells us of her experience as she walked home alone, late one night.

> 'The experience I am relating here took place in the summer. I had spent the weekend with friends and because of a sudden train strike I had to return by bus which deposited me half a mile from my home in the middle of the night: it could have been 1.30 a.m. I began to walk across the common. It was quite dark of course – street lamps had all been switched off, and there was no traffic – but the night was warm and still, and the sky full of stars. I had no particular feeling beyond a slight nervousness about being out so late in a lonely spot: on the whole, I think I was enjoying the walk.
>
> I had nearly reached my mother's house when I suddenly realised that the whole sky was alive with sound. Out of the deep silence grew a whole orchestration – not of music, but of a harmonious blending of sounds, as though an infinite number of radio transmitters were emitting signals, each one with its own unique pitch and rhythm of pulsation. There was no melody and no form: I just knew that what I was hearing was the music of the spheres, something that has no beginning and no ending, and the grandeur and simplicity of this filled me with amazement and delight. At the same time I vividly recalled the taste of painted metal and

my memory tugged me straight back to the nursery in another house, where, night after night (though I had totally forgotten it until that moment) I had stood as a tiny child, sucking the bars at the window and listening to the stars.

I arrived at my mother's house and went indoors; upstairs in my bedroom I could still hear the stars singing, and they continued to do so until I reluctantly went to sleep. I have never heard this sound again, though I have often longed to do so for the joy and satisfaction it brought. Perhaps the oddest part of this experience was that it felt so normal.

Soon afterwards, I began working on an army training film dealing with radio relay, and I took the opportunity of questioning the officer acting as adviser. He assured me that stars do in fact emit radio signals, and he explained patiently and at length why human ears are unable to receive these signals. I did not tell him of my experience – but I have shared it with friends from time to time, and one close friend told me that he had had a very similar experience late one night while serving as a naval officer in the Red Sea.'[7]

Apparently, we have now reached the age of intuition in which, becoming aware of, and understanding and using this special gift, this intuitive energy, as well as enriching our own lives, we can pass on the 'secret' to others.

Einstein, scientist, is quoted as saying, 'The only real valuable thing is intuition', and successful business people have all pointed to intuition as important to their success, while Oprah Winfrey talks about using intuition in her daily life. She has stated that her mission in life is to show people how to think differently about their lives, to open their minds and see things differently; to get in touch with the spiritual side of their nature.

When Jan didn't listen to her 'intuition', her intuitive energy, the voice in her head 'screaming' at her, as she puts it, not to get into the car as there would be a terrible accident, she ended up in hospital on a life-support machine, followed by months in hospital, as she slowly recovered from her dreadful ordeal.

The accident Jan was involved in happened years ago, but Julie's accident happened fairly recently, when she also ended up in hospital, but with minor injuries compared to what 'might have been', if she hadn't listened to the voice in her head.

She was pulling out of a supermarket car park when a huge transporter, packed with new cars, and heading towards her, signalled a move. Julies' intuition, suddenly kicking in, told her to move in a certain direction, which she did immediately, to allow the driver, as she thought room to turn; but he changed his mind, and did something different.

Julie remembers seeing him holding up his hands in horror as he realised his mistake, and if she had not followed her own intuition and moved to where she did, her car would have been sliced in two, with Julie a probable fatality.

It *was* a serious accident, with Julie having to be cut out of her car and rushed to hospital, staying in for a short time, but she made a remarkable recovery.

Julie calls it 'spiritual intervention', and she has certainly experienced plenty of that in her long life working as a medium, devoting herself to helping others, and proving 'survival' – of so-called 'death'.

Since a young girl, Julie has had an interest in the 'spirit world', and early on noticed that there were a number of things she 'foretold' that came true. She developed this interest as she grew up, and was once told that she had two guides or helpers, (from the other side of life), who have walked with her from the day she was born.

The years passed, and Julie, now happily married to George, with one son and two daughters, joined a local spiritualist church and, within six months of joining, was invited to be in their 'development' class. She soon proved her sincere love and devotion to the spirit world, always striving, as a medium, to be the best she could be, in service to the two worlds, perhaps little thinking that through 'fate'(?), or call it circumstances, she was to be called on to give a lifetime of service.

Twenty-five years ago, and two to three months before a terrible tragedy struck in her life, Julie had a private sitting with a medium away from her own church. She was delighted, but perhaps a little 'apprehensive', when the medium told her, 'You must be getting ready to work for spirit because all your guides are gathering around you.' Curious, Julie asked the medium, 'What am I going to do, when is this going to happen?' The answer: 'When the corn is ripe, you will know.' How true that message proved to be.

Julie and George enjoyed their holidays away together, in their caravan, parked at a beautiful spot up north called Bamburgh, by the sea. It soon became a favourite place, and it was on one such holiday (twenty-five years ago) when Julie, unable to sleep, and she stresses that she was *not* asleep, and it was 2.15 in the morning, heard a voice which she recognised, but the words seemed strange. 'What has to be will be, and you can't change it.'

Four days later, a Sunday, Julie and George arrived back home at 9.45, and unpacked. They were doing all the usual jobs people do after a holiday away, when George felt unwell. He had not been ill, always a healthy, fit man, but within the hour, from 9.45 p.m. to 10.45 p.m., the doctor and an ambulance, were on the scene, but it was too late. George died at home, with Julie by his side.

As she sat, alone, stunned and unbelieving, by his body, she called out to him: 'If you had said you were going to go, I would have said, "Don't go, please don't leave me, I won't let you go."' Then, in all her despair, she remembered the words she had heard so clearly spoken to her – in the night – only days before. 'What has to be will be, and you can't change it.' As she sat there, grieving, she wondered and wondered, her mind in turmoil at the terrible shock of it all.

A few days after the funeral, Julie was sitting quietly at home, alone, when the message the medium had given her some months before suddenly came into her mind; '*You must be getting ready to work for spirit because all your guides are gathering around you.*' She remembered asking, 'What…when…?' and the answer, 'When the corn is ripe, you will know.'

August 7th 1988 was the last journey home they made together. It was a beautiful day, the end of another wonderful holiday, a perfect scene, with the farmers and farm hands working flat out to gather in the harvest. She remembered how she had remarked to George, who was driving, how busy they were, and what a hard time it was for them, and she remembered feeling sorry for them, thinking about all their hard work…such a lovely scene… Thinking back, slowly, wistfully, deeply, suddenly, with a 'start', she remembered the last part of the message. The message she had received from the medium, months before: 'When the corn is ripe, you will know,' and know, she did.

• • •

When we think about it deeply, seriously, we should be able to realise the many ways in which we can be 'guided', and 'helped', through our lives, and how many of those ways emanate from our own psyche. We all know what it means to have a 'conscience', and we have thought about 'dreams' and 'coincidence' and intuition, but there are so many other ways to be looked at, to be considered – to name a few; astrology, numerology, and the great puzzler of all time – 'fate'.

Are you the sort of person who believes in 'what will be, will be', in another word 'fate'? A true fatalist believes that everything that happens in life is pre-ordained. Then there are those who accept the idea of 'fate' up to a point, but also believe in free will. 'Fate' is so 'unfathomable', we will never make true sense of it on this side of life, *if* on the other. The subject intrigues people of all races and beliefs, just as much as a rise in positive thinking about 'intuition', 'coincidence' (a coincidence, is believed to be God's way of working a miracle anonymously), 'healing', 'yoga', 'meditation', 'numerology', 'astrology', and other related subjects. The number of people interested in astrology (many reading their horoscopes as part of their daily routine), who, in turn have become fascinated by the beauty of the stars, the night sky, space, has risen dramatically over the past few years. This interest, or fascination, is possibly helped by the outstanding programmes now put out all over the world, escalating over the past decade, when serious concern over the future of our earth plane seems to be on a high. Perhaps we are now looking at 'nature', and this includes *all* living things, in a different way, a less selfish way, as we begin to realise and understand just how much we 'depend' on nature, and how much we have learnt from nature. There are scientists who would assert that we have learnt 'everything' from nature, since the beginning of time.

Are we *really* beginning at last to believe the truth, the seriousness of the words 'we don't own the planet, we share it'?

Numerology is the study of numbers and their symbolic significance – when you have an understanding of their meaning, and how they can affect the pattern of life. Steven Smith doesn't understand them, he has tried to and read about them; he certainly has an on-going relationship with them, especially the numbers 911. He told me some remarkable experiences that I included in a book I was writing at the time[8] and now a recent experience involves his wife Jane. Arriving at the car park barrier, on her way to work, Jane noticed that the number on the clock read 911. At first, she thought it was stuck on that number, but found out later that it wasn't, it just kept turning up. These numbers have certainly had great significance in Steven's life, also as 'divided' numbers, a '9', or a '1', etc. Recently, on a visit to Cyprus, where they have a holiday home, Steve and Jane met up with friends to go out for a meal at a certain restaurant, but on meeting, changed their minds and went somewhere different. The waiter at this different place showed them to their table, which, it turned out, was two tables joined together, making the number 9 &11.

Are we still thinking here about 'fate'; everything pre-ordained, or have we free will, where signs in life can be looked to as a 'guide'. Our intuition, if we take notice, is a guide; our conscience, if we listen to it, is a guide; and if we all 'took notice' of our intuition, and 'obeyed' our consciences, what a wonderful world it would be! Then we have coincidences that happen, that have been called 'God's way of working a miracle anonymously'. Would you like to sit back comfortably for a few moments, and try to recall any coincidences that have happened to you, at one time or another; coincidences that have left a mark, something that you will never forget. It may even be a coincidence that led to dramatic changes (for the better I hope) in your life, or simply to changes in your 'way of life'. Going back to the notion of 'fate' or 'free will', reading the moving words from the Bible in Ecclesiastes[9] surely gives us pause for more thought:

> 'To everything there is a season, and a time to every purpose under the heaven: A time to be born, and a time to die: a time to plant and a time to sow: a time to weep, and a time to laugh: a time to mourn, and a time to dance.'

Therefore, is it that there is definitely a time set out for us to be born, and for when we 'die', when we pass on to the higher side of life, meet our fate, make our transition, as some like to express it? In any life there is always a time to weep, and a time to laugh, a time to mourn, and a time to dance. Can we take from all this thinking and reading we have been doing about fate, that there *is* a special time, our very own special time, for birth and death? That perhaps the broad outline of our lives *is* 'laid out for us' and we fill in the rest.

With these major factors set in place, do we have free will to fill in the rest?

Do we care? Perhaps, after all, we had better leave this section of the book with the (wise?) words quoted previously, 'What will be, will be.'

There is no way we can even begin to understand 'life', as we see it, here on the earth plane, but there is one thing for sure. There is always present, always 'with us', the 'something', or 'someone', we can all 'turn to', when in trouble, desperate for help, don't know where to turn. It is a 'natural reaction' for us, for all of us, to turn to that 'inner strength', always there, even though we may have ignored it for years. It is a natural reaction, to go 'within' for help, guidance, assurance; and 'it', whatever 'it', may be (we might say God, Father God, Mother Father God; Creator, the Life Force, Universal Energy). A favourite 'prayer' or quote these days seems to be to, 'put it out to the Universe'. Does it matter about the name, title, whatever? What does matter is that the love, the help, the care and concern will always be there, freely available, for 'each and every one of us', no matter what; and all we have to do is 'ask'. Of course, we have to be able to understand the 'answers' we receive – the 'message'.

We have been promised that a spiritual teacher, seer, prophet, will be with us in this new age of ours, the Age of Aquarius, where it is prophesied that humanity will move to being a more 'spiritual'

– therefore more fulfilled, happier – society, as we realise, begin to understand, that it is 'within' that counts; it is 'within' that is our spirit. It is 'within' that makes us what we are.

'Great are they who see that the spiritual is stronger than any material force.'[10]

• • •

Shirley MacLaine, actress/film star, was on her 'spiritual quest', in a library, looking for a certain book, when one fell off a shelf and landed in front of her. It was the very one she was looking for.

There is a quote that says, 'when the pupil is ready, the teacher will appear.'

'When the corn is ripe, then you will know.'

(Or is this me getting my metaphors mixed up?!)

• • •

The new age we are now in, where the inevitable changes rule and yesterday's day belongs to the past almost at birth, sees us breathless at the speed of life, with the words 'here today gone tomorrow' probably never more true. Humanity, however, in its broadest, deepest sense, will not change. No matter in what century or age we live, there will always be that about us, some inner yearning (although often unrecognised), which will eventually lead us home.

The recent headline, Church 'is on brink of extinction', words written by the former Archbishop of Canterbury, Lord Carey, were perhaps not as shocking to readers in these turbulent times in which we live, as they would have been, say, ten to fifteen years ago. One of the reasons given for this decline in the membership of the Church of England is the failure to bring young people into the services. Numbers attending the Sunday congregations 'are quoted' as being half the numbers of the 1960s, and that going to church is not something that is natural in their lives nowadays.

Lord Carey did say, 'It is still the case that people are essentially looking for spiritual fulfilment.'

Headline, Church 'is on the brink of extinction', words written by Lord Carey.

Another headline: 'Religion is 'Dead'.

Could it be that religion is not 'dead', it has simply changed.

Jimmy had a serious drink problem for most of his long life, and every now and again the problem would 'take over', and he would sacrifice everything to 'go on the road', as they say. News of his death was especially sad for his sister Mary and niece; they were in the only car to follow the hearse. As it passed the Working Men's Club, where he had been a regular customer, during a short break in the traffic, a 'dray' pulled out and positioned itself directly behind the hearse where it stayed until they reached the crematorium.

Ironically (although by accident), a 'fitting' send off, for Jimmy.

Chapter Three

Divine Transportation

> *'And it came to pass, as they still went on, and talked, that, behold, there appeared a chariot of fire, and horses of fire, and parted them both asunder: and Elijah went up by a whirlwind into heaven.'* 11 Kings. 2-11

WHEN WE HAVE A 'so called paranormal' experience, we know that we have had one, and no one can convince us otherwise. It is as though we have a sudden 'revelation', an awareness of 'something' that may have been as nothing to us yesterday, but can become all our tomorrows.

We might find ourselves more 'understanding', 'caring', towards all forms of life. We find ourselves sensitive to all sorts of possibilities, both 'within', and in the world around; seeing things in a different light; 'lit up', exciting, transformed, as we ourselves may be transformed; recognising that 'there' for us, showing us, are 'signs', 'evidences', 'truths', that can lead us to worlds within worlds within worlds within worlds!

When people have a paranormal experience, they know they have had one, and no one can convince them otherwise.

• • •

Rosemary Brown was born on the 27th July 1916, in Balham, southwest London. She had very little musical training: in 1948, she got an upright piano and had lessons for a third time, but they usually only lasted for about a year. Yet Rosemary was unique among musicians the world over, as she was visited, encouraged, and helped to play (the piano), and *write down* compositions dictated to her by some of the 'greatest' dead composers, by the masters themselves; Liszt, Chopin, Beethoven, to name but a few.

A quiet, humble woman, born into a poor, hard-working family, she seems to be the most unlikely person to have attracted such visits. From a young age, she was always having visions, prophetic dreams, and hearing voices. She was only seven years old when she had a vision of an elderly man with long white hair wearing a black gown. He said he was Liszt. 'He told me that when I grew up, he would give me music,' she remembers.

In her book, *Immortals by My Side*,[1] Rosemary tells us, 'Mine was not a happy childhood. There were ever recurring bouts of hardship, drudgery, and the parental bullying.' She believes that she was an ordinary child, in spite of her psychic gifts; a child who longed for affection, the same as other children, and who could be naughty. Her mother taught her to pray regularly, although she did not insist that she attend Sunday school or church. However, by the time she was sixteen, Rosemary had visited many different religious centres and 'read a multitude of books about people's ideas of God'.

She worked in the civil service, married, in 1952, Charles Brown, a government scientist who had once worked as a gardener for King Farouk of Egypt, and settled happily to becoming a mother to a daughter, then a son. 'I still had no idea what was ahead of me.'

In 1961, her husband and her mother died, and it was perhaps at this point that her psychic gifts, always present and recognised, really came to the fore. Again, she had it rough; now a widow with two young children.

Her only real outside interest, at this particular time in her life, was to join a small prayer group who met in a house in South London, to pray for the sick. There was a man in the group who prophesied that within ten years she would be world-famous. Rosemary was too astonished to answer him. Fame was the last thing she wanted. She loved quietness and peaceful surroundings and to live unnoticed.

'At the time when that prophecy was made, I was a very impoverished widow struggling to bring up my two children alone. I was slaving away in school kitchens, scrubbing floors, and scouring pots to make ends meet.'

In 1964, she had an accident in the school kitchen, and once again started playing the piano during her long convalescence. It was at this time that Liszt re-appeared, as promised. She recognised him immediately. She tells us that at first, music came to her from the composers only after she had been in deep prayer, but that after she had been working with them for several years, they would appear after a brief period of inner prayer and meditation; this seeming to suffice to attune her with them.

Rosemary could see her spirit visitors quite clearly; she could describe the sound of their voices, the clothes they wore, and the conversations they had were very revealing about the spirit world and how they perceived 'our world'.

When she started to try to play, and then write down the music that they dictated to her, Liszt controlled her hands for a few bars at a time, and then she wrote the notes down. 'I seemed to lose control of my hands, it was as though someone were guiding them.' Chopin told her which notes to play and pushed her fingers down on the right keys. Beethoven and Bach liked her to sit at a table and take dictation with a pencil. Schubert tried to sing his compositions, but she said, 'He didn't have a very good voice.'

Gradually, over time, she learnt so much from them and trusted them implicitly, and it was probably through her conversations with Liszt, in particular, she discovered that their main purpose was not just to give more of their music to the world, or even to prove, to give assurance, that there is no death. The main purpose was to encourage the growing number of people who are awakening to 'deeper levels of consciousness within themselves' (here again possibly a foretelling of the spiritual revolution to come?), to understand that the rare flashes of insight into things and events they have, through this new insight, are real. That the information they may receive 'could not be had' by any of the usual means, but to 'Go Within' to find the greater truths!

In answer to a question Rosemary put to Liszt about sensing the identity of a spirit, she brought in the words 'vibrations' or 'waves'. Liszt stated that (as mentioned in an earlier chapter) each person has his or her own dynamic field, which can be 'sensed' or 'picked up', and each person's dynamic field is peculiar to that person only, in the same way that finger prints are individual. He continued, 'Could our advancing technology one day design a machine that could scan or register these dynamic fields, and perhaps even record the impact of a burglar's field to aid detection and arrest? Technology has already outstripped the limits to which the average imagination might have stretched a century ago, and its future achievements could reach beyond our wildest dreams.' (And all this from Liszt, a composer who lived from 1811 to 1886, in a conversation with Rosemary Brown, a humble housewife from Balham, southwest London, in the 1960s.)

As music happened, and evidence of the presence of dead composers visiting Rosemary Brown, and through time, other famous dead personalities visiting, came about, word spread. People of like mind, and therefore with an understanding of Rosemary's experiences, told others, and others told others until, within a year, her home was invaded by 'a cavalcade of reporters, television crews, and all manner of interested or curious folk!'

Soon, she was meeting people from all 'walks of life'. She was introduced to some of the 'well to do' – interested parties proud to be her friends – but perhaps, not so proud and friendly when, with the forthcoming fame, press, reviews, radio interviews, (including one with the BBC *Woman's Hour*), the heat was on, and she was deserted by some of those she had trusted and believed would stand by her. One such person was a Sir George Solti, and another couple, a doctor who, along with his wife who had first befriended Rosemary, and were both believers in her work/experiences. They had made such a show of wanting to help and befriend Rosemary, but at the outset of all the publicity, perhaps becoming a little flustered by it all, as she thought, Sir George, particularly, tried to advise her to be 'Secretive about the Whole Thing'. (Obviously, he was missing the point!) His secretary wrote Rosemary a strange letter saying that they could not 'afford to be involved on outer levels with these astral-level phenomena-type things'!

Rosemary: 'Then came the thunderbolt – a type of thunderbolt I was to meet again and again, when people would be convinced of the genuineness of my work, but would 'chicken out' when it came to giving any public testimony'. Realising this sort of thing – people deserting her or wavering – would happen all the time, she knew she would have to be ready to 'hold the stage' on her own, to fight a lone battle against enormous odds.

'If I did not have the courage to take a firm stand for what I believed to be true and to be of some possible value to humanity, I would be failing in my duty. I vowed in that instant to go on steadfastly with the work, come what may.'

Later, others would come and go in supporting roles of various kinds, and Sir George and the doctor and his wife, according to Rosemary, perhaps a little reassured by favourable reports through letters (probably as a result of a BBC broadcast), began to make plans of their own to present the work in a suitable form.

(At this stage, Rosemary was quite 'overwhelmed' by the enormous show of support from the public through all the letters arriving, and no one to help her to answer them.)

With the release in May 1970, by Philips, of some of the piano music, she started her serious travelling, going first to Dublin, where she took part in a live broadcast sitting next to Jackie Stewart, the champion racing driver. 'I marvelled at the quiet courage and good humour of this great driver,' and later, when she met the distinguished conductor, Colin Davis, he told her he had always thought that death meant complete annihilation, but that she had made him think again.

Rosemary made several appearances on the BBC, paid a flying visit to Paris where she had a non-stop programme of activities that included radio broadcasts, television appearances, press conferences, and her one wish granted, when she visited Chopin's grave. 'We had arranged for all that already. We wish to film you beside Chopin's tomb.'

'When I returned to England, Chopin gave me a new piece of music, a little nocturne, in commemoration of my visit. It is a poignant piece in A minor, reminiscent of the falling of raindrops or teardrops. He can even make sadness beautiful.'

Through time, film crews from all over the world, who were interested in her and her work, visited and filmed her. Her travels took her to America, where she performed at the Town Hall, in New York, and she appeared on the *Tonight Show*, with Johnny Carson. Most critics of the day agreed that Rosemary's transcriptions were much in the style of the great composers – some said they were forgeries but could not explain how she did it. The whole of the music world could not decide on what was happening. She was 'thoroughly investigated' by both musicians and psychologists, and not one could find any evidence of her cheating. In fact, after meeting her, they were all convinced of her innocence. Liszt did not reappear to her (not since she was a child) until 1964, and before this, she had little interest in music and had had the minimal instruction in it. According to one parishioner where she lived, she was useless at playing and struggled to play the simplest hymn. Using a pencil, and to everyone's amazement who later saw the transcripts, she could write down all the music given to her.

Scholars and world-famous musicians who accepted her performances and transcriptions (compositions from the dead composers) as genuine, helped to publicise this 'unbelievable phenomenon of the twentieth century', with their own performances of the music, and made arrangements for Rosemary's performances and talks, until the message was finally, and seriously, taken up throughout the world. Taken up and accepted, probably, and perhaps, because it is a common phenomenon for the ordinary human being (as indeed Rosemary was) to have dreams, visions, premonitions; to 'see' and 'hear' the so-called 'dead', but at that time 'not quite the thing to talk about'.

Rosemary Brown, however, stepped out of the 'ordinary' into the super-extra-ordinary, as she performed to packed concert halls in front of 'the experts', the critics, and not only performed, but performed with an expertise far above her ordinary ability in life. (Where do we find the endless hours, the years, of piano practice; the expert tuition, the necessary cultural background for such a massive undertaking?) Finally, perhaps the biggest mystery of all; to have received the music she played, and *wrote out* – a massive task in itself – for the world to share, from the great beyond...

The whole story really is quite unbelievable to contemplate, but it happened, and there are films, tapes, recordings, her transcripts, published works, including:

Bagatelle in E flat (Beethoven)
Grubelei (Liszt)
Moment Musical 1 (Schubert)
Waltz Brahms; all in *The Rosemary Brown Piano Album*, to prove it.

The musicologists and the critics who did not believe what they saw and heard – her performances on the piano, and the music she transcribed – admitted that they did not know how she did it, if it was fakery. 'They *liked* her and believed in her – immensely.' A famous musician and critic who slammed her work but had to admit he could accept a piece by Rachmaninoff (perhaps one of the most difficult pieces of music from the composers to play and write down). On and on it continued, but through it all, Rosemary remained a most 'liked' and respected 'lady', quite a feat to achieve in the strange circumstances in which she found herself. She held true to her belief in the work she was trying to do, and no doubt often had to 'hold the stage', as she put it, alone; fighting a 'lone battle'; but it must have pleased her to know that, in spite of all, she *was* truly liked and respected, and what better accolade.

• • •

Dreams, visions – and there *is* a difference – encounters,

coincidences, strong guiding thoughts, impressions, you might say 'feelings'; precognition – a sudden knowing of something, and intuition, are all part of the tools, the abilities, early man (and woman) were endowed with, and which they recognised as part of their make-up to help them through life. They not only hunted and fished for survival, but they looked to nature, the whole of nature, for lessons to learn.

They could tell by the feel, the 'mood' of the wind, the position and strength of the sun, the fall of the rain, how the day would progress. They could even tell what sort of a season they were likely to have. They followed the stars, looking for every nuance in the heavens to give them guidance. The rolling of the sea and the travel of the rivers, and all plant life, all of nature, was their story. Restlessness, and sudden movement among animals, taken as warning signs of possible trouble ahead, would see early man acting on these signs, even to the point of leaving their homes; moving on. Acting in all good faith that 'God', perhaps represented as the sun, or some other deity of nature, whom they worshipped and thanked for *all* things, was always there with them, as their guiding light.

(Interesting to note that here, we are talking about early man/woman, thousands of years ago; and now, in the twenty-first century, the current trend – many people being uncomfortable with the word 'God' – is to call on, and thank the Universe!)

Scientists are now beginning to accept, and make public the fact that we must take notice and learn from the natural world; nature, the animal kingdom, our feathered friends; fish, (fish *can* feel pain); every micro-tiny-mite in existence; everything has a part to play. Following on from that, science has stated the fact that it might even be through observing and acting on findings from nature, that we can save the planet. A special study has recently highlighted the wonder, the natural wonder, of a spider's web. Tougher than steel, and intricately woven, the web is resilient enough to withstand the force of hurricanes and fierce attacks from predators – and this not just because of the strength of the silk, but the clever design. So impressed are the experts by the study that they say the findings could be used to help with the design of new, unbreakable materials, and fall-safe buildings. This is only one tiny example of what we can learn from nature.

It appears to be almost impossible for us in our world today, living our lifestyle, to imagine, and compare with 'how it was' in those way-back early centuries of time. Yet there is a thread running through all the aeons of history, stretching from the very first signs of life here on the earth plane, to where we are today… to you and to me. The thread, or connection, as we might say, is 'spirit': sometimes wavering, pulling thin, then strong again, with strength unbelievable to behold, when we look at the example, the truth, preached, by the early martyrs, and indeed, martyrs throughout history, who endured, held firm, through unspeakable suffering, for their belief, when the world was perhaps forgetful of the 'word of God', and the spirit within.

From the earliest of early days, from the time of the 'ancients' (as they are sometimes called) they would have sat around the fire, recounting dreams, visions, coincidences; telling the tale of perhaps how they had been saved by a warning, a sign, their own intuition. Such things were all a natural part of life, as it was to visit a soothsayer or a (witch doctor) healer. The Bible is full of stories of the so-called-paranormal, not thought of as paranormal in biblical times, but again, part of everyday life. Stories abound of signs, and 'angels', and dreams. Many of us will know well the story of Samuel and his calling; how the word of God was 'first revealed' to him.

'The temple lamp was dimmed, and Samuel, a young boy, was 'laid down to sleep', when the Lord called, "Samuel, Samuel." Thinking it was Eli, his master, the priest, under whose tutelage he lived, he ran in to where Eli was sleeping, saying, "Here am I."

Eli told him to go back to bed, he had not called him. After this had happened for the third time, Samuel hearing his name called, and running in to Eli, the priest realised that it was God calling Samuel. He told him to answer, when it happened again, with the words, "Speak Lord, for thy servant heareth." Samuel replied to the voice when it called to him again, as Eli had instructed, and in time, after many years, and many adventures, and trials and tribulations, Samuel became one of the most revered and loved of the prophets and judges.'[2]

• • •

It would seem that the words, 'so it is and ever shall be', repeated in prayer since time immemorial, are true, and being 'proved' true today, perhaps more than ever before. We, in our modernity and hi-tech world, are not shy of recognising the existence of – even if expressed as the 'something else' – angels, guides, helpers, beings from the spirit world, the world of light. We are not shy of explaining that a coincidence (said to be God's way of working a miracle anonymously) brought about a big, wonderful change to a life; not shy of telling how a dream came true, or a 'feeling' of something about to happen 'played out' down to the last detail. Customs, little traditions: lighting prayer candles, tying a prayer/message on to a tree or leaving it with flowers by the roadside, remembering to send that special card with carefully chosen words of comfort or care; these are all new ideas wrapped up in old clothes.

Our experiences, all touching on our inner self, our true self, our spirit, the real you, the real me, the magical world, we can all tap into, when we recognise, open up, tune in, to the infinite.

• • •

'Years ago, I was living in the YWCA hostel in Banbury, Oxford. I was twenty-five years old, and it was a Saturday afternoon and

I was lying on my bed feeling depressed and lonely. I wanted to get up and go out to buy some cigarettes but I felt unable to move because of the feeling of depression. Instead, I continued to lie on the bed and began to wish fervently, and with all my strength, that I had some religion to help me.

Within a few minutes, a very bright light appeared in the opposite corner of the room near to the ceiling, and I heard a voice say, 'Take up your bed and walk.'

I am a graduate, married now to a scientist, and I have never suffered from hallucinations of any sort. I am still not particularly religious but this experience has stayed with me in complete detail for many years.'[3]

The young woman writing about the above experience 'tapped into the infinite', one Saturday afternoon, as she lay on her bed, desperate for help. When someone has a so-called, paranormal experience, they *know* they have had one, and no one can convince them otherwise.

• • •

Margaret found that an encounter she had, one ordinary night, after falling into what she thought was simply a deep sleep amazing, but with a twist at the end that she could not explain. She puzzled over it, until she finally found, and accepted the answer.

It was a night in July 2005, when Margaret, in a deep, but 'active' sleep, as she describes it, became re-united with her dead loved ones, her husband, parents, and Toby, the family 'treasure', a Yorkshire terrier. Other family members were there, but seemingly remained in the background.

'It was all so happy and busy—' her words, the ones she wrote down later '—and everything else forgotten but the joy of being together. It was talk, talk, talk, with me flitting around so excited and happy; then, in the middle of all this, I heard the doorbell ring, but I remember thinking to myself, "Who could that be at this time in the morning?" For some reason, I knew it was very early, and ignored it, just carrying on, enjoying our "togetherness". Soon after, it might even have been immediately, I heard the doorbell ring again. (Both times, the doorbell ringing was REAL, and not imagined.) The second time it rang, however, it was as if I was being woken from a very deep sleep and was too tired to be bothered about getting up to answer it.'

Still aware that it was very early in the morning, Margaret struggled, but knew she had to make the effort to get up and find out what was going on. She looked out of the window to see who it could be, but just as she had thought, no one was there. Checking the time, she found it was 6.40 a.m. Now fully awake, at first she felt 'unbalanced', a bit shaky, remembering everything very clearly and how happy it was, but then, why did it change? Why the doorbell ringing, and why did it ring twice? She puzzled about it so much that she took up a book on the meaning of dreams and sat with it trying to find an answer. She looked up 'bells' and there were entries for bells ringing, and church bells, but no, nothing on doorbells. By now, knowing how real it all was, everything that had happened, meeting up with her loved ones, and then, how daft it seemed to be sitting, early morning, reading up about doorbells ringing, she knew that she had to find an answer, which eventually, she did.

Explaining the whole thing in detail to a medium, Margaret, at first concerned, soon had the answer to the whole night's experience, including the doorbell episode, which she finally accepted. She had indeed met up with her loved ones; there was a great longing within her to do this, having lost her beloved husband only a few years earlier, but to meet with them, *she*, herself, had had to be 'taken over', taken out of her body, while in the sleep state, to visit the spirit world. The visit would have to be a short one, even though it seemed to her to be a long time, and the doorbell ringing was a sign for her to return. Ignoring s sign, the first time, it became imperative for her to return immediately, therefore the need for a second ringing, which, fortunately, she answered.

• • •

Now where (on earth) do we go from there! From a visit to the spirit world and back, and all taking place during a good night's sleep. We might try AUSTRALIA, where a beautiful little dream experience proved true the very day after it happened.

Sonia was so brave; not well herself, she and her husband moved to Australia to be near their two daughters who had settled there. Having visited, she found that the climate suited her poor health, and so they made the move. Quite tragically and unexpectedly, not long after, Fred, her husband, died, leaving Sonia, already in poor health, inconsolable except for the fact that she had great belief in 'the other side of life', and so she waited patiently for evidence of survival from Fred. Evidence soon came.

Cottesloe beach had become a favourite haunt of Sonia and Fred, and in a dream one night, not too long after he had passed away, he took her back there to watch two whales 'basking' in the sun. It was a wonderful experience for Sonia, made perfect when, on television the next evening, it was reported, as she had seen in the dream – that two whales were found 'basking' in the sun at Cottesloe beach.

• • •

Perhaps it is time now to look a little more closely, trying to understand the depth and the real significance behind the meaning of the experiences we have just been reading about, OBEs; Out of Body Experiences.

We none of us know the depth of vision, or travel, we might undertake, in the sleep state; according to one psychoanalyst, 'dreams are the hidden depth of the mind'. There are dreams –

Gary dreamt of a baby born with fingers missing and web fingers, his wife due to give birth at any time. The baby was born with web fingers.

Sarah tells us of a dream she had some years ago, where a friend called at her home, and asked her about the time of her dad's funeral (which had been two years previously). 'I asked her what she meant, and she said, "The time you left the house for the crematorium etc, because my dad has died." I woke up feeling upset because the details of the dream were so vivid, I kept on thinking about it the following day. That night, I was looking at the local paper on the internet. I looked at the Deaths and saw the announcement of my friend's dad's death. He had died about five days previously and I had not heard about it, even though they live quite near.'

There are dreams, and there are dreams that turn into true OBEs, Out of Body Experiences (within the dream state), falling into various categories. The Cottesloe beach dream, proved true the next day, we can perhaps think of as a lightweight OBE, if that is the correct expression. Deep enough to give Sonia evidence of her husband's survival and continued presence, but in view of her poor health, just the right amount of out of body travel, and depth of emotion for her nervous system to take at that time.

Margaret, in her dream, out of body experience, was 'taken over' to the other side of life to the spirit world, for a brief visit. This brief visit, was a deep, emotional, serious encounter, the physical body being strong enough and 'well enough protected' for the exchange to take place; the spirit body, all the while, safely connected to the physical body by the silver cord: 'Or ever the silver cord be loosed…' is discussed in chapter one of this book.

Margaret, enjoying, *loving,* every moment of being 'reunited' with her family, needed a firm 'push' when the time came for her to leave the world of spirit and return to the earth plane; hence the ringing of the doorbell which she heard, and ignored. It rang again; and again she heard it, loud and clear, but it was only after a desperate struggle to rouse herself from the deep sleep she was in, that she finally 'came to' enough to respond.

Whatever out of body experience we are experiencing, lightweight or deep, we must understand that to remain here, on the earth plane, our spirit body, the real 'you', the real 'me', (which is doing the out of body travelling, via the silver cord), must remain connected and return to the physical body; to be severed only at the time of death.

> 'Then shall the dust return to the earth as it was:
> and the spirit shall return to God who gave it.'

A Reiki practitioner, giving her client a run-down on what *she* had experienced during the session, and feeling quite exhilarated by it all, reported that it was an intense session with lots of colour and energy, and she felt as if she was being given a lesson, on twos; everything in twos. She went on to list them:

'Two hands, with two sets of fingers, two feet, with two sets of toes.

'There are two arms, two legs; two eyes, two lungs; two kidneys and two parts (halves) to the heart. The brain has two hemispheres – right and left. You've got your spirit, and your body.' She then went on to mention opposites, light and dark, in and out, up and down and when she mentioned 'twins', she was careful to point out that although they might be the same in body, they were different in spirit.

In explaining all this to the client in detail, and obviously puzzled as to what it could mean, she quite casually added that;

'At the end, I saw a cord on the top of your head going up and up,' (she made the arm gestures of stretching higher and higher), 'right up. I couldn't see any connection, but on the top of your head the cord was in a haze tinted with pink; hazy pink, moving, pulsating, with life.'

The practitioner had not ever heard of the 'silver cord', or of any other cord – apart from the umbilical one – attached to the body, and she did not know that the client was studying and writing about this (the silver cord) at the time.

Explanations came later, and when the excitement (for both of them) of the practitioner having *seen* the cord attached to the body quietened down, the understanding of the 'twos' became clear, of course! The lesson, or lecture, on twos of everything, was leading up to the fact (and with the cord the visible proof), that, as the practitioner had mentioned in her talk, *we* are also two. We are spiritual beings in a physical body, but are as one, while here on the earth plane.

• • •

We can all, each one of us, experience a dream, a dream/vision, or a waking/vision. The young woman, living in the YWCA Hostel in Banbury, Oxford, feeling depressed and lonely, began to wish fervently and with all her strength, that she had some religion to help her. Within minutes, a bright light appeared in the opposite corner of the room near to the ceiling, and she heard a voice say, 'Take up your bed and walk.' Her waking vision, in answer to a sincere, fervent, strong call for help, is typical of the way we can be 'pulled through' a time of real need, despair, anguish.

In such a heart-felt, desperate situation, no one is ever 'let down'; there will always be an answer somewhere, somehow. The Bible is full of stories of visions and rescues, and if we could but hear of, and process the outcomes of all the 'troubled' people there must be around in our world today, visions or no visions, we would find that, we too, in our need, are not lacking in that same divine answer to our call.

Visions, however, can be simply 'vivid dreams', brought on

perhaps, by our day-to-day activities, problems, imagination, wishes, and so we have to be mindful to analyse, think them through carefully, in order not to deceive ourselves; and 'out of body' experiences are not confined to happening only in the sleep state. They are an integral part of life when we learn how to accept and understand them.

Artists, musicians, writers, healers, are only a few of those who inspired, motivated, wanting to 'share' something uplifting, spiritual, the 'good things' of life, with others, are often taken out of themselves to achieve their aims.

John Tavener, famous composer who passed away recently at the age of sixty-nine, was such a person. He 'has been described' as a 'visionary visited by angels', saying himself that his music 'came from above' and that he had auditory visions in which the music was dictated to him.[4]

(This was the way that Rosemary Brown, discussed at the beginning of this chapter, received her piano compositions.)

It appears to be that we can touch on, or *have,* an out of body experience, any day of our lives, and not just in the sleep state. As we interact with each other and the world around us, to feel an extreme emotion, one that sets pulses racing. Perhaps through an unexpected encounter, worrying news; maybe a rush of excitement that takes us into a state of euphoria; you know, when that surge of excitement flows through you and you feel 'on top of the world'. Happy, sad, in an uncontrollable rage, or a whispering within that gives you a slightly uncomfortable (physical) feeling; is this the interplay of the physical and the spirit, the physical body and the spirit body interplaying? Something happening that affects us so strongly we are 'moved within'.

'Through the emotion of the inner self, we touch the true self'.

Are we now ready to move on to NDEs, the experiences that have been subject to so much scrutiny, inquiry, recorded, deliberated over? The evidence here, with NDEs, appears to revolve around 'going through a tunnel towards a light at the end, where loved ones are waiting'...and on recovering from this NDE, lives are changed forever, to become more caring and understanding; kinder, happier, and unafraid. NDE is a near-death experience.

Jan was the young woman we thought about, when looking at the meaning of 'intuition'. In 1986, she ignored the voice inside her head screaming at her not to get into the car, and ended up in hospital on a life support machine, having an experience that changed her life, and for which, as she proudly says, 'I have always been extremely grateful.'

With serious head injuries, as well as other injuries, Jan, following an operation, was taken immediately into intensive care, and put on a life support machine. It was while on the life support machine that she had her 'near death experience'.

Jan recalls being in a very dark place, and not being able to feel her body at all. She had no movement from arms or legs, nothing. Sensing she was in a tunnel, she then saw a light in the distance, and as she focused on this light, it gradually moved towards her, getting nearer and nearer until she saw her grandmother, hair white, radiant eyes, full of love for her, and Jan remembers that her grandmother was 'shining' in this light. Jan herself felt marvellous; she felt loved and so cared for – she was always close to her grandmother anyway – she knew that she would be OK, and nothing bad would touch her, hurt her. Trying to reach out to her grandmother, she must have been making her way to be closer to her, when suddenly, the mood changed. Seemingly, to Jan, with a very feeling, soulful expression, her grandmother placed one hand over her heart, and raised the other arm as in a 'stop' sign, telling her to 'go back, it's not your time yet'.

The light was extreme, and the visitation, as Jan calls it, left something so wonderful with her, all those years ago, that she has never forgotten, and will never forget, and for which, as she is so anxious to repeat, 'she is extremely grateful'.

There is a broad picture to a near death experience, which, in following a pattern, is remarkable in itself. The patient (often) describes going through a dark tunnel leading to a light at the end, where a kindly figure, clothed in white, shimmering robes, or loved ones, are waiting. The feeling is contented, happy, often euphoric, and unafraid.

'In the ambulance, the paramedic, Vanessa, was talking to me (Gerald) when suddenly I felt myself floating down a square tunnel lit by a bright shining light. I could see four faceless figures, dressed in nun-like habits with pointy hats, float beside me and there was a feeling of calm, as if I was suspended in a lovely dream. I was looking ahead at what I thought was a large garden when suddenly everything went into reverse and I was speeding backwards through the tunnel and I was awake.'

Gerald was in hospital for six days after apparently suffering a heart attack and 'dying' for five minutes in the ambulance. When he returned home, he continued to see visions of the nuns at the foot of his bed every night for about six weeks, and said he felt their presence very comforting. 'I used to be afraid of dying alone, but I'm not anymore.'

Another important feature of an NDE is the way it changes lives for the better. Too many report the remarkable change for it to be 'ignored'. Reporting feeling better in themselves, happier, unafraid, appreciating life, not taking it all for granted, and being more caring and understanding of others. That seems to be the broad picture of a near death experience.

Dr Penny Sartori has been researching NDEs for some years, and her case studies make fascinating reading.[5] In particular, she reveals how children, as young as six months old, can have such experiences. Researchers documenting a case in the medical journal, *Critical Care Medicine*, kept in touch with the parents of a six-month old boy who had nearly died in hospital during a serious illness. Three years later, that same child, when told by his parents that his grandmother was dying, had just one question. Was she going through the tunnel to meet God? Parents of other very young children have reported similar experiences. One writer, knowledgeable about experiences of this kind, tells us that all near-death experiences are dramatic, in that those involved have approached, or even gone past the 'final frontier', before returning to this world.

Have you had a near death experience, or an out of body experience? Would you talk about it if you had? Not so long ago, an NED 'would not be talked about', and certainly not discussed openly. However, along with the many other changes we are finding in life, this subject, the so-called 'paranormal', is no longer thought about so much as 'paranormal'; it is now being seen as an *understanding of life,* with which, in all its fullness and richness, we are *all* truly blessed; whether we understand it, or try to understand it, or not.

Near- death experiences can be a message, a sign. Our lives are full of messages and signs, both in the material world and in the world of spirit. And Dr Sartori informs us that the biggest thing she realised, as a result of undertaking her research into the near death experience, is that 'by trying to pathologise these experiences, we are missing a very important point, the *message*, of the NDE. That people who *have* an NDE are usually profoundly transformed, and have much to teach us about life. They realise that we are all 'interconnected', and what we do to others, ultimately, we do to ourselves. This is the Golden Rule – treat others, as you would wish to be treated yourself, which is, as Dr Sartori points out, at the heart of all of the wisdom traditions

'In everything therefore, treat people the same way you want them to treat you.'[6]

Messages for us, signs; they are there, happening all the time, there for all of us! Can you remember when the last message/ sign, came to you? Maybe by way of a coincidence; a coincidence, remember, is God's way of working a miracle anonymously; or did it come to you by way of a dream, or an 'out of the blue' experience that changed everything? The messages, the signs, are always there for you and me; we just have to 'pick them up'. They have always been there, and will always be there; and when we recognise them, that will be when we become 'aware'. Countless people now speak about an 'angel helper', and say to another, who is perhaps having a difficult time; 'ask your angel/ helper to help you'; or they quote the now well-used expression, 'put it out to the universe'. Signs are becoming more prominent in lives, and it is often surprising to see the response, or hear it said, from people you would not think 'thought' that way, that they too have a sign, or some relevant token, to rely on.

A sign can be anything from a colour, to a number, to a (yes, you've got it) a dream; a so-called 'deceased' relative or friend, strongly entering the mind, is often enough for someone to know that there is a reason for this, and to wonder 'why'. Missing a certain bus or train some- times sets off a thought pattern such as, 'now why did I do that?' and when, as has happened on occasions, a person has been saved from a serious accident, or worse, because of missing say, a planned journey, well! Enough said.

Years ago, Susan, a great believer in the power of prayer, and the other side of life, discovered that the sign of a peacock was somehow special for her.

During a troubled time in her life, when she had a lot happening, including travelling widely, she heard about having a 'sign', and the help it could give, knowing there was a guiding influence with you, from the other side of life, caring and letting you know – by this sign – that you are never alone. And it worked! If ever she felt a bit lost, did not know which way to turn, what to do, she would do as she had always done; pray about it. But now, as well as her prayers, she had her sign, which always turned up, was always there for her, never let her down. This discovery of a sign has been steadfast to the point of 'unbelievable', for Susan. It has presented itself in so many different ways over the years that she has never ceased to be amazed at the ingenuity, the persistence, and the love she has felt from this special help she can visibly see is there for her, and for every one of us, if we did but know.

Right on time, just when needed, a peacock card (the sign) would arrive for her, and from people who did not know the significance. Once in a bathroom with large mirrors, the mirrors steamed up (after a hot shower), and this occurred at a particularly hard time of great strain and worry for Susan, the pattern caused by the steam turning into a perfect picture of a peacock. Another time, a beautiful peacock feather, enclosed in a Christmas card, arrived for her, the sender having no idea of the circumstances at the time, and the great need!

Recently, going to hospital for a check-up (and nervous of medical appointments – some call it 'white coat syndrome'), Susan, sitting in the taxi, commented quietly to her sister-in-law that she was fine about going, but she hadn't had any sign or mention of a peacock, adding, 'Probably I don't need it.' They were having a conversation about the changes made at the hospital, with its new extensions, the lay-out of the grounds, many improvements. As the taxi stopped, and Susan stepped out, the taxi driver, who had not been in on any of the conversation, called out to her while pointing a finger, 'The old Peacock Building is still over there!'

Our part in this amazing interaction with spirit, on receiving help and guidance, along with the certainty that, whatever we are facing, we are not facing alone, is to be sure that we give thanks for any help received. To give it out 'loud and clear', with a sincere, and loving heart: to 'Father God', 'Mother/Father God', the 'Universe', the unnamed 'Something', 'Creator', or whatever…

• • •

The King James Bible, still often referred to as the Book of Books, portrayed as it is in beautiful literature, is teeming with accounts of miracles, heroic deeds, mystery, myths; advice on day-to-day morality, stories of heaven and hell, and it is also beset with signs and warnings. From the well-loved story's we have heard since childhood:-

> The shepherds watching their flock by night when an angel appeared telling them of the birth of a Saviour: 'And this shall be a sign unto you, you shall find the babe wrapped in swaddling clothes, lying in a manger.'[7] To the story of the wise men, following the star: 'When they saw the star they rejoiced with exceeding great joy'[8] and they followed the star to Bethlehem where the baby lay; and later, being warned in a dream that they should not return to tell King Herod (about the birth), they departed into their own country a different way.[9]

– to the less well known; but they are all there, along with everything we want to know and need to know to live by; our moral code, as the saying goes; the stories and the signs, running throughout the Bible from beginning to end, emphasising the ways that God can (and still does) communicate with us mere mortals.

The Bible's King Solomon, was a great and wise ruler, who was determined to build the finest Temple, House of God, ever. With a great gathering of silver, stone and cedarwood, and precious stones, still ships sailed to other lands, seeking out yet more treasures with which to adorn the building, which took seven years to build, and all for the worship of God. The finest of robes made, and beautiful ceremonies planned, for the first ceremony and consecration, during which, as it tells us in the Bible, God gave a visible sign of His favour.

> It came to pass, that the priests, and the tribes, with their sons and their brethren, being arrayed in white linen, having cymbals and psalteries and harps; the trumpeters and singers, stood at the east end of the altar, and with them a hundred and twenty priests, were as one, to make one sound to be heard in praising and thanking the Lord, saying, 'For he is good; for his mercy endureth for ever: that then the house was filled with a cloud; for the glory of the Lord had filled the house of God. 'God being praised, giveth a visible sign of his favour. [10]

At this time, as our world is in need of good, strong leadership to take us through the unsettling period we are living in, and as we struggle to make our way through these unsettling times (having just moved into The Age of Aquarius), is it that the new players (leaders) are already being placed (put in position). With one, at least, heralded, not by a fanfare of trumpets, but by a bolt of lightning! Are there really strong signs and signals hitting us from…somewhere?

A photograph of a bolt of lightning showed it appearing to strike St Peter's Basilica on the same day that Pope Benedict XVI announced his resignation, stunning the world. The date was 11th February 2013. It is being said by some senior figures in the church to be a sign from God. The feeling seems to be that *now* is the time for the church to move ahead. 'Something important is about to happen. We shouldn't be afraid because when God is present, we should be full of hope and confidence that something important, great, is going to happen for the church and for the world!'

Apparently, Pope Benedict, who is now devoting his life to a time of prayer and study, had a mystical experience that led him to resign. His decision was the result of divine inspiration; and now (and so quickly), the wonders that the Holy Spirit is doing through his successor, Pope Francis, have made him realise that his decision to resign was 'the will of God'.

Just read the newspaper articles with headlines such as 'Francis effect pulls crowds back to church'; 'Pope Idol'; 'Is the Francis effect the miracle the Church needs?' and 'It's like he has put his arms around us all and drawn us all back.'

Pope Francis is the charismatic and 'special' one, chosen to lead millions of people all over the world, and accepted not only by Catholics. He has already, in the months since his succession, made great strides in his desire to help, heal, and be a leader who can inspire all people to think of the 'spiritual' as the reality, and the only way to a happy, fulfilling, life.

Pope Francis, helping, healing, inspiring, millions more who are Catholics…millions, who are of other faiths; and the millions who have no faith but in life itself!

• • •

Over the last experiences we have thought about, encompassing signs, and warnings, and omens, we have visited, through the Bible, the majesty, the grandeur, of kings. The three wise men, who were the three kings in the well-loved story of how they followed the star to Bethlehem, and the baby Jesus. We have felt the splendour of King Solomon, the great and wise ruler who put 'everything', time, money, riches, 'love', into building the best ever Temple, House of God, for the Lord. We then thought of our two modern-day Popes, Benedict and Francis, who, in the brilliance, and sanctity of their abode, The Vatican, St Peter's Basilica, Rome, have recently 'enthralled' us with their story of resignation and succession, divine inspiration, and a 'calling' to lead our troubled world into calmer waters.

This chapter has given a lot of thought to the signs and warnings and omens that are there, and have always been there, since the beginning. Freely given, and given equally to each and every one of us, and all we have to do is say: yes, we can ask, but then we have to be 'aware'. No matter how we address this undying love, this help, this comfort, this sustenance that is there for us – 'God', Universal Energy', the 'Unnamed Something' – it is there, and we never forget when we have called on that help, whatever our need; and we never forget that it has never let us down.

(The knock on the door, the ring of the bell, showing someone cares.)

• • •

In the winter of 2013, at about the Christmas time, Jane, who lives in Somerset, had an outstanding show of support from the other side of life, and just at the right time; it was something she badly needed. She was 'visited' on three occasions by three (different) butterflies. They were colourful, and full of life, as each one circled around and around her home until she opened the door, and let them out to freedom, all this happening in the middle of winter. Even more remarkable was the fact that the third butterfly flew around, then landed on her heart. Sensitive and caring to the needs of all nature, Jane felt the love and encouragement in this action, and gave 'thanks'.

Not long after, bending down to pick up a tennis ball from the ground, during a game, she was surprised to find a butterfly perched it. Her instinctive reaction was to say, 'Oh hello, it's you again', as she picked up the ball, and off it flew. She no doubt thought (though not perhaps in these words), 'Message received!'

Grandma Norah was quite startled when her three and a half year old granddaughter, Grace, who is obviously learning a lot at her nursery school, asked her, 'Do you know Jesus?' Norah (after a long, thoughtful pause) answered, 'Yes,' then waited for a reply. She waited and waited; another long pause, then Grace finally answered, 'He died.'

A few weeks later she informed Norah, 'He is alive again now.'

Chapter Four

An Awakening of Understanding

> *'And I say unto you, ask, and it shall be given you; seek, and*
> *ye shall find;*
> *Knock, and it shall be opened unto you.*
> *For everyone that asketh receiveth; and he that seeketh findeth;*
> *and to him*
> *that knocketh it shall be opened.'*[1]

THIS IS THE NEW Age of Aquarius, and a spiritual revolution is forecast, when we will return to our spiritual roots. Our New Age surging along with all the new technology, is not, however, hindering our spiritual progress, but accompanying it, and why not say it? – 'The Spiritual is leading the way.'

Thinking it over carefully, with all the, as it seems, 'gradually imposed' changes to our lives you will read about in this chapter, is it not as though some superior (is it really invisible?) power is at work?

'Spiritual Law is superior to material law.'

All the time there are hints, little pushes, shoves in some cases, moving closer, interacting freely in the everyday, very ordinary lives of the very ordinary Jack and Jill around the world – yes, you and me again, pointing out to us all, showing us a better way. The other side of life is moving in closer, encouraging us to 'go within', yet again giving us a firm reminder that we are spiritual beings in a physical body, living in a material world.

• • •

Pauline and her mother carried a sadness with them over years at the passing of Pauline's brother Joseph, when Pauline was only sixteen. A sadness that was only finally lifted with a comfort found in a way they would have never expected. Here is Pauline's story, and it concerns her son Ray, now eleven years old, but who was three and a half at the time.

> (August 2012)
> Ray was in the back of the car, his dad was driving, when Ray started laughing and pulling silly faces and waving. It was at the time he was learning the alphabet (he was an avid fan of *Countdown*); anyway, when my husband asked him what he was laughing at, he said the initials, 'J O S'. When they got to the top of our farm track, he waved and said, 'Bye bye.' My husband, who is a very down to earth person and doesn't believe in anything supernatural, rang me straightaway to tell me. The thing is, my brother passed away when I was sixteen and although he was called Joseph, we all called

him 'Jos'. When my husband told me, I thought it just must have been a huge coincidence.

A few days later, we were all in the car together, and at the same point, my son started laughing and pulling faces again. I asked him what he was doing and he pointed to the sky and said the initials J O S again. When we got to the top of the lane, he said, 'Bye bye.' This went on for about three months, on and off, and always at the same point in the road. It's funny but although my husband was 'freaked out', it gave me and my mum a lot of comfort. After about three months, it suddenly stopped.

Nothing like that has ever happened to us before and my son didn't know anything about Jos as we had never mentioned him as Ray was so young. *That incident has made me think more about things.*

'That incident has made me think more about things.' How many times have we heard those words and how many times have they applied to ourselves, and how many times have the answers been forthcoming in the most extraordinary ways?

'Seek and you shall find; Ask and it shall be given you.'

(Going into the library looking for a book on spirituality and one falls off the shelf landing at your feet – Shirley Maclaine's experience.)

It took a tragedy in the life of Justin Welby, the new Archbishop of Canterbury, to give him the assurance, perhaps the strength he needed, to pursue a call from God. Over the years, he served various parishes, and worked in the community, devoting his life to helping others and doing reconciliation work, setting up teams to help people in bereavement, baptisms, in hospitals. Through his involvement, numbers in church going started to increase. Again, as with the new Pope Frances, is it that he is the right man in the right place at the right time, for this new, spiritual age we are now in? Thinking again about the Age of Aquarius, often called the New Age, which writer Marilyn Ferguson sums up as 'power changing hands, from dying hierarchies to living networks'. In other words, 'people power'.

The forecast (hope) behind the New Age is that there will be a great outpouring of human potential – physical, intellectual, creative and spiritual – remembering the meaning of spiritual as to 'love', to 'care'.

'And now faith, hope, and love abide, these three;
and the greatest of these is love.'

A great outpouring of human potential and there will be a development of resources previously unknown, bringing in nature, or unrecognised resources...a drug, based on a 400-year-old herbal gout remedy, could be effective on a range of cancers. Early tests show it is effective, zapping cancer without harming healthy cells. Clinical trials are due to start in months, and Professor Laurence Patterson of Bradford University, said: 'We are very excited about this.'[2]

The forecast tells us that we will begin to recognise our earth plane, the *whole* of the Universe, as being one complete source of living intelligence that we must live with (this is starting to happen) in harmony, rather than in a relationship of use and abuse, understanding that – to repeat – we are the partners, not the owners in creation.

'A human consciousness is tapping into the global consciousness of our planet, bringing about a new spiritual awareness.'[3]

Are we now really witnessing the start of a spiritual revolution (moving alongside the technical revolution, or the other way around), with the promise of a teacher, a prophet, a seer, to come? This is the Age of Aquarius, often called the New Age.

Andrew, eleven years old, had only been out metal detecting with his dad twice, when he uncovered a new but badly damaged I phone, deeply embedded in the sand. On returning home, he casually remarked to his mother, 'That's the best day of my metal detecting life.'

Now immersed as we are, in new technology, older people are even asking their five-year-olds how to do 'such and such' on their mobile phones or the internet. We have gone from the Walkman of a few years ago – with 'music on the move', constant 'sound' of one sort or another – to the I phone to keep us up to date with 'everything'; but as you read these words, technology will have moved way beyond our understanding at this moment, and even beyond the comprehension of many scientists.

> (Stop Press!) Technical information of 2014. (OXOOOOOOOA OX3O4 546O2, OXOOOOOO1C, OXOOO). Beginning dump of physical memory Physical memory dump complete. Contact your system administrator or technical support group for further assistance.

Get the drift? We spiritual beings that we all are, are living in this material world…whey hey, needles and pins… loop the loop, and all that jazz… (and on it goes).

Science is even now pondering on the thought that being too deeply engaged, and for too long, in technology, with all the energies involved, is probably not good for the physical. Children in particular, immersed, as so many of them are, in and around all these energies – waves – sound bands – electronics, are vulnerable, and tests are only now starting to be carried out with the young ones, to discover any detrimental effects there may be in so much exposure. Only time will tell.

Our two worlds (the other side of life and the earth plane) are coming closer every day, and we, all of us, can notice this as we hear comments in everyday encounters indicating an understanding that we are no longer afraid to voice.

Edith, who we mentioned in an earlier chapter and who is naturally clairvoyant, and has been since childhood, was watching television recently, and turned to find her mother (who passed over years ago) sitting beside her on the sofa. She was delighted but a bit shocked at the way it happened, wondering why! Knowing well that there must have been a reason, and still puzzling over her appearance, it was only later that she realised that the day was her mother's birthday.

Is it not surprising to find that the word 'paranormal' is now being questioned as never before by countless people who understand and accept the so-called 'paranormal' as a 'natural' part of life. Understanding the fact that our inner being, our spirit, is our driving force, our main stay in life *is* who we are.

A taxi driver in Las Vegas, talking openly to his passengers about his life, his heartaches and worries, but how that, now, positive changes for him and his family urged him to speak of the strangeness but wonderfulness of life, he exclaimed fervently as they were leaving him, 'Dreams do come true.' So it is not surprising, is it, in our world today, that our great need is to find the spiritual side of life emerge strongly, to chivvy us, to push us, to lead us out of all the chaos, the mayhem, the self-destructiveness we are witnessing all around us, everywhere in the world? Self-destructiveness is driven by those who are power-mad, greedy for all for material gain. But things, they are a-changing, and just as it says in the Bible:

'The people that walked in darkness have seen a great light.'[4]

So, too, have we seen the light. In the deep darkness of our world, today, we are beginning to see the light, the light of change, bringing with it the certainty of hope, as more and more of us, of like minds, are bonding together. There are groups of people, worldwide, with similar feelings, ideas, interests, beliefs, encouraging each other, waking up to the fact that we are, first and foremost, spirit. We are realising that we are spiritual beings, needing to be fed spiritual nourishment, and all that implies. We are spiritual beings residing in a physical body, with the opportunity, through our knowledge, our faith, our belief in our inner being as the true self, to achieve our best potential, to be the best we can, for each other, and for the world, of which of course, we are a part.

Being in touch with spirit certainly does not exclude having a sense of humour and a bit of fun.

Shirley, not quite knowing what to think or what to believe, as she smelt her mother's perfume in the morning, when she woke up, told her husband before he went downstairs to make a cup of tea – he soon returned, telling her, 'Well, she's been here and put the kettle on. It was hot!' (There was no one else in the house.)

Ranulph Fiennes, one of the world's greatest living explorers, in his new book *Cold*, describes how he saved the life of his friend Mike Stroud, on their attempt to ski across the Arctic unaided, in 1992. Ranulph was in the lead and well away; he writes in the book that it was his policy never to look back, but on this occasion, he did. Something prompted him, told him, to turn around, and as he did so he was just in time to see that his friend was in serious trouble. Prompt action saved Mike. Years later, on another expedition, this same, strong, tough explorer told how, in a particularly desperate situation, he turned to prayer for help... 'I prayed hard,' and an hour later, his prayer was answered.[5]

The Bible (again): 'God is our refuge and strength, an ever present help in times of trouble.'[6]

Let's sum up with the words of another man also going

through a particularly difficult time: 'It's at times like these when we realise how lucky we are to have God.'

• • •

Now let's look at the bigger picture of life, that bigger picture, *the world*, as a community; is it mainly because of the new technology that we are coming together, closer than ever before? If we are going to have a spiritual revolution, then surely it must be 'worldwide', and there are strong signs that it is. According to one writer, 'Religious systems [of the world] are travelling in the direction of pure ethnic morals; a moral code or moral questions with religion becoming a standard of conduct,' while Spirituality remains, as always, spiritual.

The passing of Nelson Mandela, the leader, known, respected, and loved *everywhere,* just about brought the world to a standstill when, although expected for a long time, his departure from this life left us, in some strange way, feeling 'bereft'. And who could be more suitable, and what better words could be spoken to sum up his life than the words of Archbishop Desmond Tutu, spoken just after Mandela's death:

> God, thank you for the gift of Madiba. Thank you for what he has enabled us to know we can become. Help us to become that kind of nation.

Those words were spoken so sincerely, so sensitively, and so beautifully, and as reported so simply, in one major newspaper: **'The World Listened'.**

The world listened, and the world is ready for the changes now coming in, thick and fast. Have you noticed, all across the globe, the way dictators are gradually being silenced or ousted, in favour of a more 'gentle', caring, and fairer form of authority? We think here, particularly, of Aung San Suu Kyi, the Burmese opposition leader. Suu Kyi, who has suffered fifteen years of house arrest, the cruel loss of her husband, enforced isolation, yet she has managed to survive and to 'never give up', and to have her voice (for the people) heard. Unbelievable as it has seemed, even after so many years, there is now the possibility of her gaining power, although perhaps, still far off. 'Clear winds of change are blowing through Burma,' said an official, 'and there is a positive change but nobody knows how far it will go.' – This from a diplomat. The Red Cross 'has been granted access to prisons', all death sentences have been commuted, and 20,000 prisoners freed from 'prisons and labour camps'. The cruelty and tyranny has been 'toned down'.

It appears to be that clear winds of change are blowing throughout the world, as we witness the struggle, striving, and positive rise of people everywhere for 'justice', equality, and a weeding out of those who have, until now, remained safe in their own comfort zone, while dishing out hell to everyone else, i.e. dictators of one sort or another!

There is an old saying that something 'good' always comes out of a 'sad' or 'bad' situation, and this has certainly proved true in the dreadful disasters we have faced in recent years. Time after time we have seen citizens of the world rise above politics, monetary concerns, social inequalities, religious differences, rise above all obstacles, to pull together in a show of unity perhaps never before witnessed, through floods, earthquakes, fires, storms, one disaster after another, somewhere.

'In our world, we make the impossible possible' – an advert for some new form of technology, but it could well apply here to an air disaster, where it seems the impossible was also possible in a disaster in March of this year, 2014, the disappearance of Flight MH370. It was thought to be almost impossible – we are back to the best in modern technology again – for an aeroplane of this size (239 passengers and crew, a regular, well-controlled take-off), apparently, in practically no time, to disappear; after months of searching, there is still no definite news of what happened at the time of writing.

As I write these words, we are waiting for information on the shocking tragedy of yet another Malaysian plane, Flight MH17, which crashed on July 17, 2014, with the loss of 298 passengers, many of them children. The world now waits, watches 'with a quietness', a 'hushed reverence', yet at the same time an ever-growing fear, at the possibility, the probability, that it was a man-made catastrophe.[7]

Still awaiting news of what could have happened to Flight MH370, the horrendous scenes of anguish suffered by the loved ones, as viewed by the world, and over weeks of continual news coverage (due to the strange circumstances of the disaster), were at times difficult to take. Yet the response by the world was quite wondrous to behold in the way that everyone, from everywhere, appeared to be *willing* the aircraft to be found – with all on board safe and well. Not only willing it to be found, the world is getting on out there to help in whatever way possible. Yet again, no questions asked, with overriding bureaucracy ignored, all red tape abolished, as ordinary people, citizens of the world, simply want to help, are determined to help, make their voices heard. Individuals, small, poor countries, offer services; rich nations, with no 'second thoughts', send out equipment, rescue boats, staff; all offer the help of *anything;* the forefront of technology on the move, with the best in man-power…and the prayers! Oh, the prayers, the love pouring out, to passengers and desperate relatives alike, and to the scores of brave, 'would-be' rescuers. ('It's at times like these when we realise how lucky we are to have God.') The response to this disaster was truly astonishing to watch, to read about, to listen to. It brought a lump to the throat and tears to the eyes. We have heard plenty about man's inhumanity to man, let us celebrate, rejoice, waving our arms high up in the air in salute to man's care, love, sacrifice *for* humanity.

Now, all over the world, people are coming together in a show of unity for the common good. Coming together as communities, as groups, even the children, everyone is working together to help each other in these swiftly changing times in which we live. The street children in Delhi, taking things out of the hands of government officials, are determined to change things. They have bonded together and started a newspaper written for other, younger street children; it started with writing by hand on scraps of paper then passed around as news, messages, all over the city. They stuck at it, and gradually, with help and admiration from adults, it is growing and turning into a successful endeavour.

There has been a stirring amongst the young in the poorer parts of Africa. The ones who have been lucky enough to have some sort of an education are grouping together, forming small societies, and spreading the word around, encouraging others to start their own schools for the young; and it is working – people power, children power!

In Soweto, South Africa, a charity has been set up to help poor children (hopefully saving them from a life of crime), to help those who have nothing but a talent to develop that talent! Already, lives have been 'changed'. While in the Gold Coast, West Africa, teenagers have organised a 'child parliament' to help children who are in a desperate plight, the teenagers simply taking things into their own hands, feeling that they have to do *something* to help the children in their own country.

In America, and the idea is moving on to other countries, helping people through the recent (and still?) years of austerity, are 'Food Trucks'. Hundreds of these trucks are travelling through America, aiming for the poorest areas, carrying a great choice of the best food, and catering for different nationalities. People can eat well and cheaply with this innovative 'Street Food', to give it its name. The trucks carry all the necessary equipment for a kitchen; fridges, ovens, grills, and they even ask the communities they visit to put forward any new recipes. These food trucks have been not only a life-saver for countless people, but a winner in the way of innovation and quality of goods; food coming straight from the farmers, and with no packaging or frills to pay for. (In Los Angeles, pop-up restaurants are appearing here and there; little shops that just open now and again for diners.)

It would appear that everywhere, especially over the last difficult years, difficult and almost impossible financially for so many people worldwide, there are so many not just coming forward but 'rushing' forward to be of assistance and give of their time, expertise, and often money. The wealthiest among us are giving more and pledging more of their fortune to charity, encouraging others to do the same. Named the 'Giving Pledge', it has apparently spread internationally from its roots in America, and in 2013, more British donors were making this pledge.

Giving, caring, sharing, volunteering, people who selflessly *give,* back to the community…could this all be part of the spiritual revolution we hear about? There is a boom in spiritual choirs, the interest in these found in schools as well as churches, and a lot of inspiration, hope and love coming from the message of the gospel choirs, more popular than ever. Schools, believing in the need, in our hectic world, to 'calm' the children – there is too much shouting going on – are setting time aside to practise a little 'meditation'; and it works! In February 2014, there was an announcement that the Girl Guides can keep the name of God in their pledge! (Apparently there was a move to take it out!!)

The BBC programme, SOS, The Big Build, helps families who have run into trouble trying to improve their homes – deserving cases, helped by the community, all the trades people coming together to work for the family, and what a marvellous, uplifting programme, the gratitude knowing no bounds.

Have *you* noticed the gradual changes in programmes on TV, on the radio, and reporting in the press? There seems to be a constant asking for *our* thoughts, *our* feelings, *our* ideas, on just about everything. 'Have you a story you would like to tell?' 'A problem to share (with the rest of the viewers, listeners); can we have your opinion on?' There seems to be more audience participation programmes such as quiz shows, with the prize money going to charity. Countless numbers of people are taking on all sorts of challenges, new challenges, and *all* for charity; and, in spite of the dreadful hardship many of these same people doing the challenges have faced, or are still facing, there has probably never before been seen, and on such a large scale, more generosity of spirit.

There is a continual appearance of yet more 'discussion groups', debating, question and answer sessions, on the airwaves, as well as down at the pub, in the community centre, covering all social and political issues possible. First-time and often extraordinarily creative (small) businesses are springing up; new ideas, new 'thinking', new opinions are being sought after from, yes, the likes of you, and me; is it really starting to feel that somehow, authority, the establishment (and has this been 'forced' to happen?) is at last listening, and wanting to hear what the ordinary citizens have to say?

People power – it is everywhere! Helping on the land, in the country, by the sea – working, volunteering, spending every spare moment to preserve, protect, our Victorian piers, our trees, nature everywhere, our wildlife, architecture, history. Socially, among scores of other plans to develop a more 'caring community', there are 'friends of prisoners' for all crimes. In housing, there is a move to make available as flats or houses buildings connected with the high street (unused shops or businesses), and all rundown properties in the area; to re-open where possible, as well as for business, shops (and libraries and schools) for people to meet socially. There is a move to encourage more of us (amateurs) to help in science, observing, recording, making notes on weather, earth tremors, nature, people observing from home, in their own area, partaking, in the new technology in the sciences, in astrology, and much more besides.

Beth is only one, and a typical example, of the countless helpers in all communities. She does a sterling job, allowing and encouraging her New Age shop, Holistic Harmony, a 'Mind Body and Spirit' shop, in the north of England, to be used as a 'go-between', a sort of pick-up point for various organisations and charities, and it all started with a chat with a stranger at a Christmas dinner two years ago. Ann, the 'stranger' sitting next to Beth at the dinner, runs a project to help people who find themselves in all manner of difficult circumstances, and the project welcomes donations of any kind. It runs a food bank, and helps with the re-housing of homeless people – amongst other things. Beth was asked if she would help by collecting items in her shop, such as coats, gloves, and scarves. People responded immediately, soon starting to donate more and more; stuff arrived, specified items, and much more besides. A chance conversation Beth had with a volunteer from the local St Cuthbert's church led to *them* taking items to Beth's shop, Holistic Harmony. The show of kindness was amazing, but leaving Beth at a loss as to what to do, how to cope with this mass of generosity.

Such is life – the very ordinary life of you and me, and now it seems that, in these new times in which we are living, business life is also being 'pushed and pulled, persuaded' that there *is*, there really *is*, always time to care. A magazine featuring the power of correct business procedures writes that, 'Most businesses are hierarchical and based on fear. They miss out on revenue because they think there isn't time to care,' and the question posed is: 'If bossing people around isn't the best way to get them to perform, is the answer to combine work with well-being?' The article continues with answers such as letting employees feel valued, motivated – not just used and pushed around, but listened to, praised, sharing, encouraged to 'give back'! Another idea, around for a few years now, is for a 'quiet room or space' to be available for employees to have a little time to themselves, if needed, perhaps for personal reasons, or for meditation, or to pray. The last two are being made available, apparently, more than realised.

An announcement just made on the radio, as I am writing these words, is to inform businesses of a special conference to discuss the relevance of using philosophy in their work etiquette.

Thinking deeply about it, with all these apparent 'gradually imposed' changes to our lives, is it not as though some superior – (is it really an invisible?) power is at work? 'Spiritual law is superior to material law.'[8] Hints, little pushes, shoves in some cases, move us closer, interacting, flowing freely, in the everyday, very ordinary lives of the very ordinary, worldwide Jack and Jill (yes, you and me again), pointing out to us all a better way.

No draughts, no window open, but a photograph floats off a shelf to land in front of you. The sudden scent of flowers, or perfume; the smell of tobacco when none is around, but the quick 'whiff' is enough to grab your attention, then gone, disappeared, as if it had never been; but you know that it was there! The dream you could not stop thinking about and puzzling over. Why? The telephone call you wondered about (for a long time), questioning within yourself *why* had it not happened, and then, as it came into your mind, just at that particular moment, 'Ring, ring!' A touch on the shoulder, yet no one there. A coldness, never felt before, that you sense as a presence, yet you are not afraid, merely questioning. Your subconscious telling you, not to do 'such and such a thing', while in another instance, your intuition races with encouragement to 'Yes, go for it!'

The other side of life comes in closer, perhaps to make us think and give us a reminder that we are spiritual (to be spiritual is to love, to care) beings in a physical body, living in a material world.

Two ladies were overheard talking at a bus stop, one greatly excited because she had just heard, on the radio, as she was leaving home, a song that meant a lot to her and her husband, and the day was the actual tenth anniversary of his passing. Even the sombre, dampening effect of the other 'lady' – obviously not too impressed by the tale, could not deflate her, as she kept up the same theme, sitting there together, after boarding the bus. Her thrill at hearing that special song, and on the very day of the anniversary of her husband's passing, continued, then, as if reflecting on her friend's disinterest (or disbelief), ended it all triumphantly with, 'Well, whatever, it certainly lifted me.'

Those words, 'Well, whatever, it certainly lifted me,' reminded me of words written on a slate, hanging in a garden centre.

> 'People may forget what you said and what you did,
> but they will never forget how you made them feel.'

So it is, with the contacts we are 'privileged' to receive from the world of spirit. We will never forget the photograph floating off a shelf to land in front of us; a burst of perfume, the smell of tobacco, the touch on the shoulder, the special song heard, and on the special day. We will never forget the countless, mesmerizing, other ways…of spirit…because of the way they make us 'feel'; uplifted, excited, HAPPY, belonging, yes; 'part of', yes; that there really is, a loving, caring 'something', whatever the name, and that, wherever we go, whatever we do, there always will be.

Not too many years ago, but now thought of by many as old-fashioned times, ancient even (mentioned in an earlier chapter – another world, which to be truthful it was), proudly hanging up in many homes were texts, usually of a religious nature. The words, often beautifully, lovingly hand-stitched, or woven in colourful wools, or copied out by hand – calligraphy being very popular. One of the favourites was, 'HOME SWEET HOME'; then there were a variety of others such as, 'IN EVERYTHING GIVE THANKS',[9] 'GOD WORKS ALL THINGS TOGETHER FOR GOOD',[10] 'BE STILL AND KNOW THAT I AM GOD', 'BE HAPPY IN THE LORD.' Those were the days of regular church-going (when it was 'the thing' to go to church, and to *be seen* going to church). Sunday school was a 'must', and a vital, often undervalued part of society.

Have we now picked up on the idea, the 'thinking' behind those old texts; same meaning, but now presented in a different way, (and still acting as a sort of 'moral guide), yet in tune with our new age. Clothes often have tiny labels sewn in: 'Happy thoughts day'; 'Be Happy'; 'Have a nice day'. Tops with boldly printed slogans such as 'We are Forever' the huge letters sometimes emblazoned in silver, are very striking. Inside the neck of another top, which the wearer only noticed when taking it off, were the words, 'Lotta Love', giving cause for a smile and a lift to the wearer…opening the package of a new purchase, a card inside with the words, 'Did we make you feel great today?' There are hundreds of things like this posted every day on twitter and Facebook.

Cushions and slates (to hang up) have followed on from the old texts that were so popular hanging up in many homes, while causing much amusement among shoppers, to give out a moral message too!

'If it howls, feed it.' 'If it cries, love it'…and under the heading 'House Rules' we read: 'If you drop it, pick it up'; 'If you sleep in it, make it up'; 'If you open it, close it'; 'Say please and thank you'. Texts, sayings, on just about everything; 'Give hugs and kisses'; 'Play nice and work hard'; 'Dream Big'; 'Laugh and Learn'; 'Share smiles and forgive'; 'Be honest and love one another', with TLC, 'Tender Loving Care' now a familiar term of usage in our vocabulary.

Many of the sayings could have almost been taken straight from the Bible, and they are everywhere – on posters, tea towels, fridge magnets, food packages, ornaments, mirrors, everywhere.

> Life is about finding yourself,
> Life is about creating yourself,
> Love what you do.

Have you noticed, in all our thinking and exploring over the last few pages, how life is moving? Have you noticed how it is taking us closer to the 'inner' side of our nature? With such thoughts and feelings, with the 'positive' swirling all around us, encompassing us, we *respond* to this caring, helping, changing, bolstering, the uplifting, encouragement; the chance to *be,* to *feel* worthwhile; we know we are in the realm of the spiritual.

Over the last few years in particular, and all over the world, there is a 'sifting out' – and this covering **all** areas of life – a sifting out, a clearing out, and a determination to get to the bottom, to the truth of crimes committed; injustice, *any* wrong doing, even the crimes of the past.

The Prime Minister, David Cameron, has issued a call to church leaders to talk on morality – morally right or wrong, not just for finance, but morality returning 'seriously'.

No one can ignore, deny, or be oblivious to the momentous changes the world is facing, and is it that a clean sweep is necessary, instigated worldwide, to coincide with the changes? Will it open doors for the move *to* a more open, caring, transparent and inclusive society, born from the chaos of NOW?! ... (And we had better get it right this time!)

Referring back to considering life as we know it, and the ways in which it is taking us, and seems to be directing us, to remember the 'inner' side of our nature, our 'spirit', how can we find the true you, the true me? How can we, in what way is it possible, for us to realise this truth? To so many of us, the physical, in all its glory, is still the absolute reality, and yet, even then, is there not that little yearning within, that little whisper from time to time, that makes us question? There is a 'something within' that demands our attention, refusing to be ignored, as if to say, 'I am here.' Is conscience not a good example? Or perhaps a sudden feeling, emotion, thought?! Thoughts are living things. The power of thought, tested and proved, emanates from the spirit, from our spirit. There are those who have actually felt their spirit *move*, but what about the rest of us...? Just touch on this phenomenon, and on the way we too can be aware of our true selves, a small example of how we can be taken to our 'inner' self.

Joan, a friend of mine, talked to me recently about suddenly losing herself in thought, while out cycling. She doesn't usually cycle too far – but the past year has been a difficult and worrying time for her, and on this particular ride, she was surprised to find that she had travelled much further than usual, without even noticing. Such is the power of thought.

Can you recall the last time you had a similar experience, becoming lost in thought (but maybe not on a bike)? I know I can, often!

Thoughts; the gateway to the inner self, often seen as the background to reality, but in truth, they *are* reality, as, touching our deeper than deep moments, we begin to understand the meaning behind sayings such as:

'Life consists of what we are thinking of all day.'[11]
'Life is what our thoughts make of it.'[12]

'As we think, so we are'; and these words, the words of the great poet, William Wordsworth, express in *one line,* emotions, tangible feelings – love, beauty, thankfulness, joy, great happiness, fear, remorse, horror, worry, tragedy, repentance, sadness –

'Thoughts that do often lie too deep for tears.' We read, and we understand.

• • •

How do you live in your thought world? This is the same question asked over the centuries by the 'wise' ones from every country and faith in the world. It was the inspired one, Gautama, the Buddha, who said, 'The mind is everything: what you think you become.'[13]

Now, in our twenty-first century, at last accepting the truth of those words, we are also emphasising the need to be positive in what we do, or aim to do. The word 'positive', as opposed to 'negative', is now another common term in our vocabulary; but do we fully understand the consequences of this truth?

> 'In your thoughts and in your conversation never dwell upon the negative side. Don't talk of sickness and disease. Talk of things that will make people better for listening to you. To dwell upon the negative side is always destructive.'[14]

Words written in 1897, referring particularly to bodily health and vigour, but we now, having finally caught on, realise they really refer to everything. The author, Ralph Waldo Trine, continues, informing us:

> 'The time will come when the work of the physician will not be to treat and attempt to heal the body, but to heal the mind, which in turn will heal the body. In other words, the true "physician" will be a teacher; his work will be to keep people well, instead of attempting to make them well after sickness and disease comes on.'[15]

Those words, explaining the idea behind 'keeping people well', free from disease, are of course, referring, also, to other things, to 'positive' thinking; but his words are certainly proving true now, as the emphasis in medicine is moving to prevention rather than cure. Trine tells us that 'every thought is a force that goes out', and, going along with his thinking, if we could but 'see' what we could achieve, personally, by 'right thinking', we would be amazed.

Science now accepts, and is on course to further promote the reality of 'thought power', having used it on patients who have false limbs, *with success!* Headlines in a popular daily newspaper state that 'Positive thinking may help the agony of arthritis', continuing with, 'Tackling the way the mind deals with pain may be as effective as anti-inflammatory drugs.' A continuing theme among the 'powers that be', although it is stressed this is 'way into the future', is 'travel by thought'. Beam me up, Scottie may not be so daft after all.

Communicating with each other by thought, as happens in the spirit world, is definitely on the science agenda; however, in thinking about it, how often does it not already happen? How many times have we said, or heard it said – he/she reacted in pure astonishment at the sudden, 'absolutely out of the blue', appearance of a person just thought about; and there are millions of other examples of the same sort of thing happening, many with seriously high implications. Nothing should surprise us! Australia has just announced its programme to use 'drones', unmanned aircraft, to deliver goods, packages, to outlying communities, but mainly to develop its use specifically for times of disaster and emergencies; and it may not be too long before we have driverless cars scattering the population; 'that's progress', as the song says. In the words of an old Arabic saying, 'Nothing is certain, and everything is possible.' How true.

• • •

The time will come when the work of the physician will be to 'heal the mind', which in turn will heal the body; and one of the evidences we have of the truth of those words is in seeing so many more of us – and worldwide – turning to the powerful, yet easily practised 'magic', called meditation. Just as the physical body needs rest, relaxation, sleep, so too does the mind, pounded as it is with all the stresses and strains of modern living. It seems that there are now more stress-related illnesses reported than ever before, and so serious is the problem that there are a growing number of institutions, including prisons and schools, turning to the proven success of meditation – and now we hear a lot about another form of 'positive thinking', 'mindfulness'.

Margaret is more than grateful for what meditation has done for her; she practises TM, Transcendental Meditation, twenty minutes, twice a day, and calls it her 'medication', so powerful has it proved to be in her life. It came to her, years ago, not only recommended by her doctor, but insisted on (knowing the difficulties she was facing), as he had witnessed personally the tremendous effect. TM is probably the easiest of all the meditations there are out there to practise. Brought to worldwide attention by the Beatles, in their heyday in the sixties, as they followed the teaching of Maharishi Mahesh Yogi, who was the founder, and who introduced it to the western world. TM does not focus on chanting or breathing like other forms of meditation. Instead, it encourages a restful state of mind beyond thinking, sitting quietly in a comfortable chair.

Benefits shown by scientific research include: TM helps alleviate stress, reduces anxiety, and improves sleep, memory, energy, creativity, intelligence; it helps reduce blood pressure, relieves fatigue, and anger; reverses ageing.

There are scores, hundreds, of ways to practise meditation, and if you are interested, it is really a matter of finding the right one for you. (This could be an instance of 'ask and ye shall receive'.)

If you are seriously interested in 'giving it a go' – meditation or mindfulness – try first what we have just been thinking about, 'the power of thought'. 'Ask and you shall receive.' Send your thoughts out to be guided to the right method for you and be alert to any responses you *will* receive. They may not happen immediately, but keep your request at the back of your mind, and follow any leads, such as: an advert in a magazine that seems to 'jump out at you', a chat along those lines, a film or discussion overheard pointing to…and so on. (As a little starter, and having asked, you are now reading these words, and they are mentioning that 'the library' is a good source of information!)

As we have been considering in this book (and he calls it a quiet revolution), thirty-nine-year-old American politician Tim Ryan gives us, in a magazine article, the headline 'The New Age is Now'. He follows up with telling us about his thirty-minute meditation ritual each morning, slowing his breathing and clearing his head of clutter. In a press interview, Tim Ryan, from Ohio, talks about the state of the world – politicians from every country not being able to see things 'quite clearly', and a lack of vision worldwide, resulting in mistrust between nations, unnecessary wars, starvation, destruction of the planet. He is pushing (in America) for a school curriculum called SEL (social, emotional learning), teaching youngsters to relax, calming themselves into a state where they are better able to learn; and he is introducing a bill to help states to implement SEL; to promote 'mindfulness' in medical schools, in teacher training programmes, and to help treat veterans. 'It's happening now,' he says, 'in the military and the prisons.' (According to the magazine *Psychology Today,* almost 10 million Americans practise some sort of meditation.)

Meditation, Mindfulness, the New Age; not coming *to* us, but *with* us; as if we didn't already know!

Under yet another heading, 'Meditation for Professionals', we read that neurologists and psychologists, are proving the benefits of meditation for life and for work, and then, 'It is said to boost brain power, produce faster thinking, better decision-making, problem-solving and creative thought.'

With celebrities getting in on the act (many celebrities have already been practising meditation – and yoga, for years), and with their numbers increasing every day, they are calling themselves 'The Millennials', the new Meditation Generation, and it has been suggested that if they needed a poster girl, then it would be Daisy Lowe, model and actress. 'I do it [meditation] morning and evening, for twenty minutes, wherever I am; on the bed or the sofa; in the garden with my little Maltese, Monty; in cars, on trains or planes,' reports Kate Spicer from *The Sunday Times*. Daisy Lowe concludes the article with: 'I like to think that I would have still turned to it in the 1970s, but if we didn't have technology, I wouldn't feel that need to have quiet time, because most of the time, let's face it, I'm on Instagram.'

• • •

Before turning to the next page (you might have noticed that there are only blank pages left in this chapter anyway), would you like to – if you are 'in the mood', and time and circumstances allow – try a little experiment. Try a gentle form of meditation, a taster if you like, and if you are unable to try this now, but you *would* like to try it, keep it in mind for a later date.

For those of you who are continuing, 'seriously', here we go. Please do not turn over to the blank pages yet!

Sit alone, quietly, in a comfortable chair – and it doesn't matter if you fall asleep while trying this 'experiment'. Away from noise, ticking clocks, ringing phones (or outside noises if possible); forget yesterday, and tomorrow, and remember there is only 'now'; sinking deeper into your chair, relax, taking deep, slow, breaths.

Follow your breathing – be aware of it; deep, slow, breaths; remember there is no hurry.

Follow your breathing, be aware of it, aware of your deep, slow, breathing continuing, slowly, deeply, as you relax into the 'silence'. There is no hurry.

Still aware of your deep, slow, breathing, 'listen' to the silence'. Listen…Listen…

Be aware of the silence (it can be very loud); take your time, there is no hurry.

Listen to your inner voice, it too can be very loud; stay aware of your deep, slow, breathing, relax…day-dream… have a catnap.

Later, when you do turn over the page to the blank pages (*but not yet*), turn over the page *slowly*, to the blank ones, always breathing slowly and deeply, always 'aware' of your breathing. Cast your eyes across the page from side to side, always slowly, as if following lines of words, but they will be *your* words, *your* thoughts, or perhaps no words, no thoughts, as you simply gaze, eyes moving *slowly*, from side to side, across the page.

Sitting quietly and comfortably, breathing slowly, breathing deeply, you are creeping, ever deeper, into 'silence'.

Relax in the 'now', deeper in the silence, no thoughts, perhaps daydreams……………aware of 'within'.

Relax *into*; scan the pages (*but not yet*) – slowly, from side to side; breathing slowly, breathing deeply, following your breathing, aware of it...

In the silence, in the calmness *you* have created, move ever deeper within, relaxed, now ready to turn, slowly, to the first of the blank pages. Thank you,

MARY

The clock on All Saints Church in Sudbury, Suffolk, began to strike thirteen at the end of January 2009. Neither the vicar nor the clock engineers could explain why the 130-year-old clock was striking the extra hour, believed to be a bad omen. The vicar said that the clock struck thirteen shortly after he joined the parish, some four years ago.

Chapter Five

The Complete (Total) Self

'Man shall not live by bread alone.' Matthew 4-4

THE EVOLVING OF A spiritual awakening along with a great burst of human potential, physical and intellectual, and with the development of resources we never knew we had, is all forecast to happen, and all happening now. A new, caring and sharing worldwide, with the Pope calling for a coming together of all faiths, all people, in prayer, for our world is all happening as forecast; and happening now.

We, you and I, are witnessing this coming together, this 'caring and sharing' worldwide, and with a new accountability (in every sense of the word), as never seen before.

WWI, France 1917

Arthur Smith needed help from his Bible for a big decision he had to make. Badly wounded in the foot, the surgeon had given him until the next day to decide if he wanted his foot left on, in which case he might get blood poisoning, or have it taken off, but that would be the end of his war service. Turning to his Bible, no doubt with a prayer in his heart, he opened it at random to find the following words staring back at him:

'The Lord shall be thy confidence, and shall keep thy foot from being taken.' Proverbs 3-26

Arthur refused the operation, surviving to write his memoirs.[1]

In the old days (and in *real* time not so long ago), it was the thing to have a Bible somewhere in the home, often on a little table or shelf at the side of the bed, or perhaps in the press (cupboard) for easy reach and 'consultation'. There was, as there had been down the centuries, a time for turning to the Bible for words of wisdom and advice, and in times of trouble, for comfort and strength – and it worked.

Would we now, in our new, ultra-modern world, find such as this? A young soldier in 1916 at the end of the battle for Mametz Wood in France, lay wounded, alone, for two days, with a Bible sticking out of his breast pocket. Finally he was found by another soldier who, before going to seek help to carry him to safety, gave him a Bible verse to ponder:

'I will never leave thee nor forsake thee.' Hebrews 13-5

Strange as it may seem, it appears to be that 'yes we would' find many of us in today's modern world who would indeed seek help and solace from the 'spiritual' (Bible), as a heading in a newspaper of 2014 tells us:

'Onward, Christian Soldiers: troops turn to religion.'[2]

Testimonies to the spiritual experiences of soldiers facing death or injury on the front line in Afghanistan, in 2011-12, range from how they prayed while under fire and carried crucifixes, Bibles and rosary beads, to one soldier seeing a shadow of the Virgin Mary during sentry duty. Another wounded soldier felt the presence of a 'protective figure' as he was 'evacuated', describing the presence as 'indescribable warmth through my body and a strange sense of peace'.

Although there is still controversy over the 'Angel of Mons' story from 1914, the start of the First World War, no one can deny the evidence of the nurses who testified to never having seen such peace, almost happiness, on the faces of the wounded and dying men brought into the field hospital on that fateful day.[3]

An article in the newspaper – of 2014 – gives us interesting glimpses into the state of mind of many of our soldiers of today, from reading about 'prayers pinned to the wall of a forward operating base, to one soldier writing Bible references on his knee pads.

The Rev Peter King described an Easter service in a cookhouse with about 100 men. They sang hymns, twenty-five received 'communion', and several had rosaries and holy medals to be 'blessed'. One soldier asked to be 'baptised' and the minister, completely convinced of his sincerity, used his helmet for the font. Many of the soldiers said that they prayed while they were in Afghanistan, and that they carried or wore a symbol of faith, and one carried his grand-father's crucifix from the Second World War. Almost seventeen percent said they felt an awareness of the presence of God. Eleven described having religious experiences, while one described seeing a shadow on the floor of the Virgin Mary praying.

These stories (testimonies), along with many others, published by The Rev Peter King, army chaplain, as part of research to investigate if soldiers in extreme danger turned to religion, and it seems that they did.

• • •

To change the mood a little, and put us in a 'lighter' frame of mind with regard to the Bible, can I tell you of an incident that I witnessed recently on a bus, which came about because of a Bible reading.

On a recent visit to London, travelling on a fairly crowded bus along Oxford Street (at a snail's pace), a well-dressed woman about forty, suddenly, and I do mean suddenly, jumped up from her window seat, then, standing by the window, opened her Bible. She stood smartly, head held high, and started reading from it, out loud, in a clear, strong voice, giving us full chapter and verse as she persevered on – and on – and on. The passengers listened quietly, politely. It was teatime and so most of them would be tired, making their way home from work, but still they listened politely. It would have been a good idea, if she had kept to a few, perhaps, more suitable, verses, giving us a 'thought for the day'...but no, the 'hell and damnation' and whatever else she came out with, it seemed that the more attentively we listened, the more drama was in the voice.

Then, just as 'suddenly' as she had jumped up from her seat and started her 'oratory', there came a loud thumping and banging and shouting from upstairs. Remember, we are still on a bus – a double-decker (obviously) – when another woman half fell down the whole flight (of stairs) in her temper and determination to get this 'bible pusher' – 'thumper' – (many unintelligible words) – to 'Shut Up! The 'screaming', shut up, SHUT Up, with flailing arms and by now expended 'pent-up exhaustion' had absolutely no effect on the reader who continued her 'spiel' without a flicker of fear or emotion or intention of 'shutting up'; she had not yet reached the end of the chapter.

Other, semi-interested passengers, maybe encouraged the reader with their complete silence through all this 'hullaballoo', while the driver, quietly and patiently, continued driving, stopping and starting with the regular flow of the other traffic; would-be passengers scrambling to get on at every opportunity, and not many appearing to 'get off'. (It was all too good to miss.) Ignored, the 'lady' protestor furiously returned to her seat upstairs (I wondered what they were all thinking up there) – but not for long. Soon, she was back again, hurtling down the stairs, looking as if, this time, she would 'throttle' the Bible reader, but she didn't. Instead, after more screaming and shouting, she approached the poor driver, demanding that he get out of his cab and 'do something' about this 'unwanted disturbance' in a public place (or words to that effect) – like, 'PUT THE BIBLE READER OFF THE BUS!' Interestingly, it was then that the passengers responded, demanding (still politely) that the reader be allowed to continue (actually, she had not stopped). In all the noise and chaos, she pluckily kept going, never wavering, and so we continued with chapter and verse, the protestor returning – again – to her seat upstairs, and me again wondering, what *were* they all thinking up there.

A quiet ten minutes or so returned, and just as we were all, newcomers, and old hands alike, beginning to quite enjoy, and be 'soothed', by the recital, listening and 'taking in' the wisdom from the Bible (whether we wanted to or not), the screaming and shouting returned. Almost 'flying', down the stairs this time, the protestor, still completely ignored by the reader (who continued with not a falter in her voice) and passengers alike, made again to confront the driver. The driver, who by this time had had enough, stopped the bus. Slowly and deliberately stepping out of his 'cab', and with one gentle 'swoop' of his arm, he carefully shepherded the protesting woman to the nearest exit, where she silently, and was it really 'complacently' descended, slipping quickly away into the darkness of the night. Meanwhile the reader continued reading, and the listeners continued listening. This is not a 'tall story', it is a true one.

• • •

2011 saw the celebration of the 400th anniversary of the publication of the King James Bible (often called The Book of Books), and the enormity of its influence on today's world; not only in spreading the Christian message, but also in the wider world of literature, history, social justice and science. It is a 'moral compass' for us in life, and in considering its influence on all of us, we need look no further than the ordinary, everyday expressions we use, to name just a few;

Oh God
Nothing new under the sun
How are the mighty fallen
Sowing seeds
Let there be light
Thank Heaven
Heaven sent
Pray for me

A day at a time
A coat of many colours
Am I my brother's keeper?
Thank God…(used regularly in conversation)
God Bless You

And here – a tiny example of things we say, perhaps not just as expressions, but as 'wisdom' for life;

It's the small things that count[4]
Do not be deceived by appearances[5]
Giving 'hope'; (to have hope)[6]
What goes around, comes around[7]
Time and chance happen to all, rich and poor alike[8]
Ask your angel to help you; we all have a guardian angel.[9]
God works all things together for good[10]
(This last one is hotly disputed more times than we will ever know, but also, perhaps more often than not, proved, with the passing of time, to be true.)

Without realising it, the Bible is with us in our everyday lives, much more than we imagine, and certainly much more often than at the usual ceremonies – the christenings, weddings, funerals, and other ceremonials we attend. It forms part of our everyday speech, as already mentioned; we think on its wisdom in times of need, and it is something that we will turn to, in one way or another, along with a prayer, when we are in trouble. There is an inbred sense of 'security' about having a Bible around, even with those who have not been particularly encouraged to see it as an 'essential' part of life, it is still 'viewed' as something 'different'; something 'special', to be quiet around – or that we should seem to be (meaning reverend), even if not understanding why. It is the

Bible. It is by far the bestselling book of all time, with the best adventure stories, mystery and romance, portraying every human emotion and experience it is possible to have – and it is all ours. It belongs to each one of us, and if we but knew it, is our helper, our comforter, friend, and guide, in life.

Stories from the Bible, enacted at church, school, theatre, movies, have always been popular (Have you got a favourite bible story? I bet you have.) and we love the foretelling, the excitement, of disasters, earthquakes, floods, and the anticipation...Jesus turning the water into wine at the wedding in Canaa, the story of the widow's mite, the promise of a prophet, a teacher, to come (we still await the prophet forecast for our new Age of Aquarius to appear). Now Hollywood has returned to the Bible epics, costing millions to make, because of popular demand after the success of the 1950s' classics such as *The Ten Commandments*, *Ben-Hur*, *Samson and Delilah* and *The King of Kings*. Recently a US series, in ten-parts, *The Bible*, attracted the largest audience of the year, and film studios are now producing stories, from the Bible, with titles such as *Exodus*, *Noah*, *God and Kings*, and the story of David, the young warrior who slew the giant Goliath, and who became King of Israel for forty years. These are stories the public want on screen, seemingly stories with a 'message', a 'spiritual theme' wrapped up in there somewhere, and not only from the Bible, but with all the new technology available out there, stories appearing to move, more than ever, into the realm of the 'paranormal' – so called!

With the latest technology, the film *Gravity* (in 3D), set us in a wonder world of space travel almost impossible to believe, except that the magic was 'We Were There'! We *moved* with the astronaut. We were flying; we twirled, and spun, way out in space, at times scared. Encompassed as we were in all the 'tricks', the manoeuvres, of the cameras, it was easy to forget all else in the 'thrill of the moment'; but the twist towards the end, gave a real, excellent showing of the 'paranormal'. Believable, and at its best, and for me, it was the icing on the cake.

We, in our *very* material world, look for *more* on the spiritual side of life, be it ghost stories (true ones of course), in fact anything that is 'truthful' about the other side of life, the spirit world. We try to understand, and learn about 'energies', as we try to do with the technology we are personally engaged in (and trying to realise, to understand, that living things, every living thing, is energy; *'we are energy'*). To understand time, and time travel; we know there is no time in the spirit world. 'Thought!' The power of – only comparatively recently been accepted as a reality – the power of healing that we have read about in the Bible; those wondrous stories that happened for real. The badly disabled man let down through the roof, on a mattress, into a room where Jesus was healing, and the words spoken to him by Jesus, 'Take up your bed and walk.' The blind man, made to see, the healing of a leper; and now, healing is happening, on the streets, all over the world, and as churches have at last awoken to its relevance, here, now, in our communities. Faith healing, spirit healing, absent healing, 'ENERGY HEALING', and the 'Healing Minute', worldwide, we are all invited to be part of at 10.00 a.m., and 10 p.m. every day.

Some of the Bible stories, thought of by many to be rather far-fetched, exaggerated, and even untrue, are now, partly due to new technology, being accepted as plausible and probably true. Look back to chapter one of this book and read again about the parting of the Red Sea, one of the most dramatic episodes in the Old Testament.

Along with the wealth of happy, good news, exciting, mysterious stories in the Bible, there are pages and pages of the fate to be 'handed out' to those who do not 'heed the word' (of God), to try to live a good, clean life, be an exemplary citizen, and so on. They are quite frightening, these pages of hell and damnation; and just a little side thought, Ronnie Kray of the infamous gang, the Kray Brothers, had a 'well thumbed' King James Bible in his possession while serving his life sentence in prison. Chapters on judgement and 'damnation' were apparently well marked.

• • •

Years ago, especially it seems, during the times of the Great Depression, there was much hardship, poverty, unbelievably dreadful living conditions, and a big drink problem, with threats of 'hell and damnation' employed at every opportunity to curb this disease. Anita talks of her grandfather, a man she only knew as the kindest, most caring soul you could ever wish to meet. This was in the '30s, but this same man had previously in his life been a terrible drunkard. He had been 'a drunkard and a violent man who would sell the furniture to get money for drink'. He was ill in hospital, and when he returned home, Anita's mother told her 'he was completely changed and never took another drink'. The change was amazing, and when his family asked 'what had changed him', he said that when he was ill and delirious, he had passed over into spirit, and was shown what was waiting for him if he didn't change his ways. He never did tell what he had seen, but it was enough to change him, according to Anita, into the wonderful man she always knew and loved.

The influence of the Bible on all our lives is immeasurable. In this chapter, we have considered its effect, in only a small way, recalling only a fraction of its message, a message to our 'inner self', encouraging, compelling, 'willing' us to *'heed'* the inner, the true, our 'spirit'. Always encouraging us to be 'happy', to aim for the best and 'make' the best of ourselves, the Bible encourages us to use the talents that we all have to give us a happy, fulfilling, life, and therefore also help towards the greater good (which in turn will make us happy). We *can* be true, and noble, and great, if we are 'true to ourselves'; true to that 'inner self', always remembering we are spiritual beings in a physical body, living in a material world.

> 'While we look not at the things which are seen, but at the things which are not seen: for the things which are seen are temporal; but the things which are not seen are eternal.'
>
> Cor 2 ch 4 v18

Still considering the effect of the Bible on our lives now, today, in the twenty-first century, the effect of its power on us through music is well 'demonstrated'. The science of music is spiritual, illusive, ethereal, and, partnered with the beauty and rich and eloquent language of the Bible, we have more than 'a song to remember'. Yet again, the following examples are just a tiny pick of the material to choose from as we further look at the power of the Bible on our lives today through music. There could well be more than one of your favourite pieces here.

Music inspired by words from the Bible:

From the story of Adam and Eve: 'When you walk in the garden', Genesis

'The Green Leaves of Summer'; 'To everything there is a season, a time to be born…and a time to die' Eccles 3

'Joseph and his coat of many colours', the story made into a musical and also a big hit for Dolly Parton, country and western star.

The Rolling Stones… 'The devil went down to Georgia' and 'Sympathy for the Devil'.

71° North Cape.
The Northern Lights in all their glory, photos taken from the mail ship Hurtigruten, *Norway – or to give them their proper name, the* Aurora Borealis.

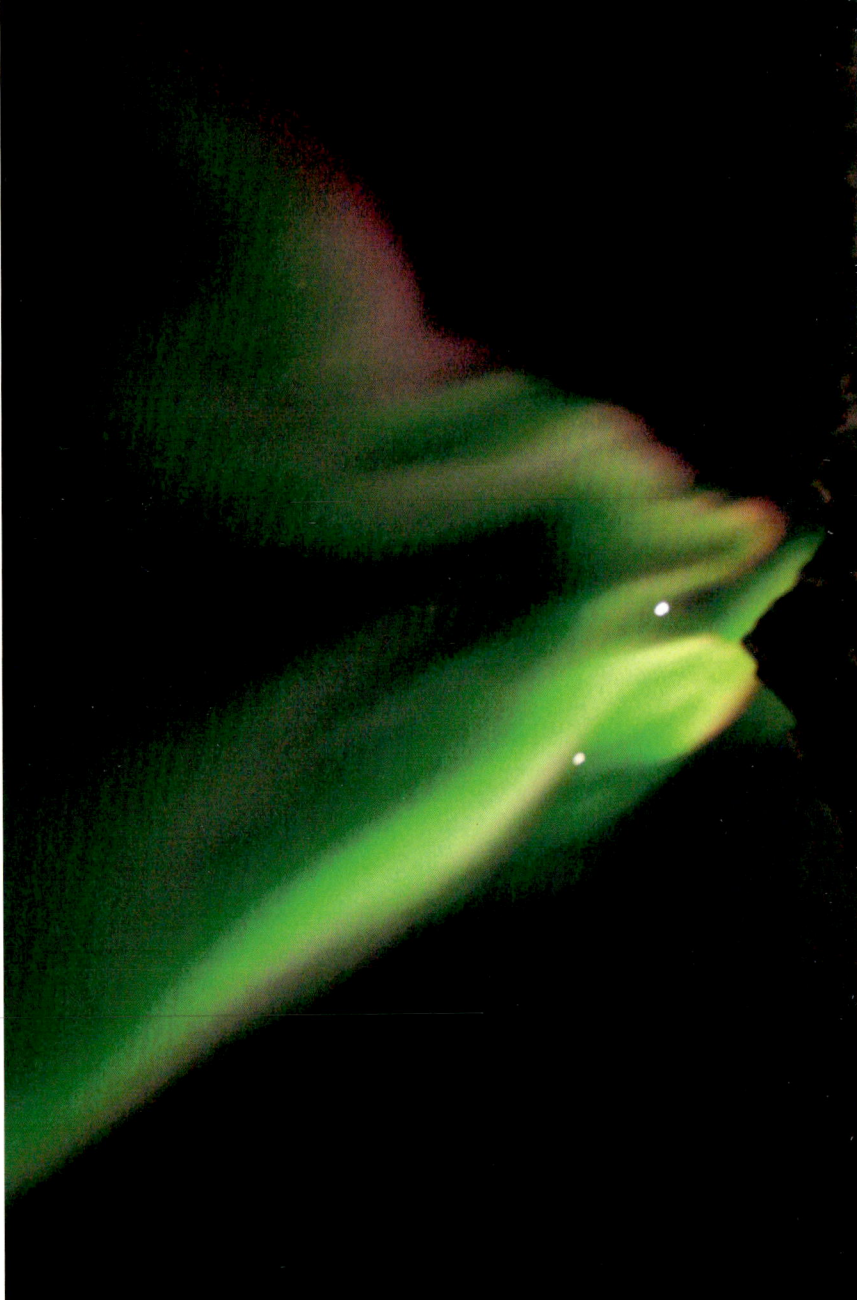

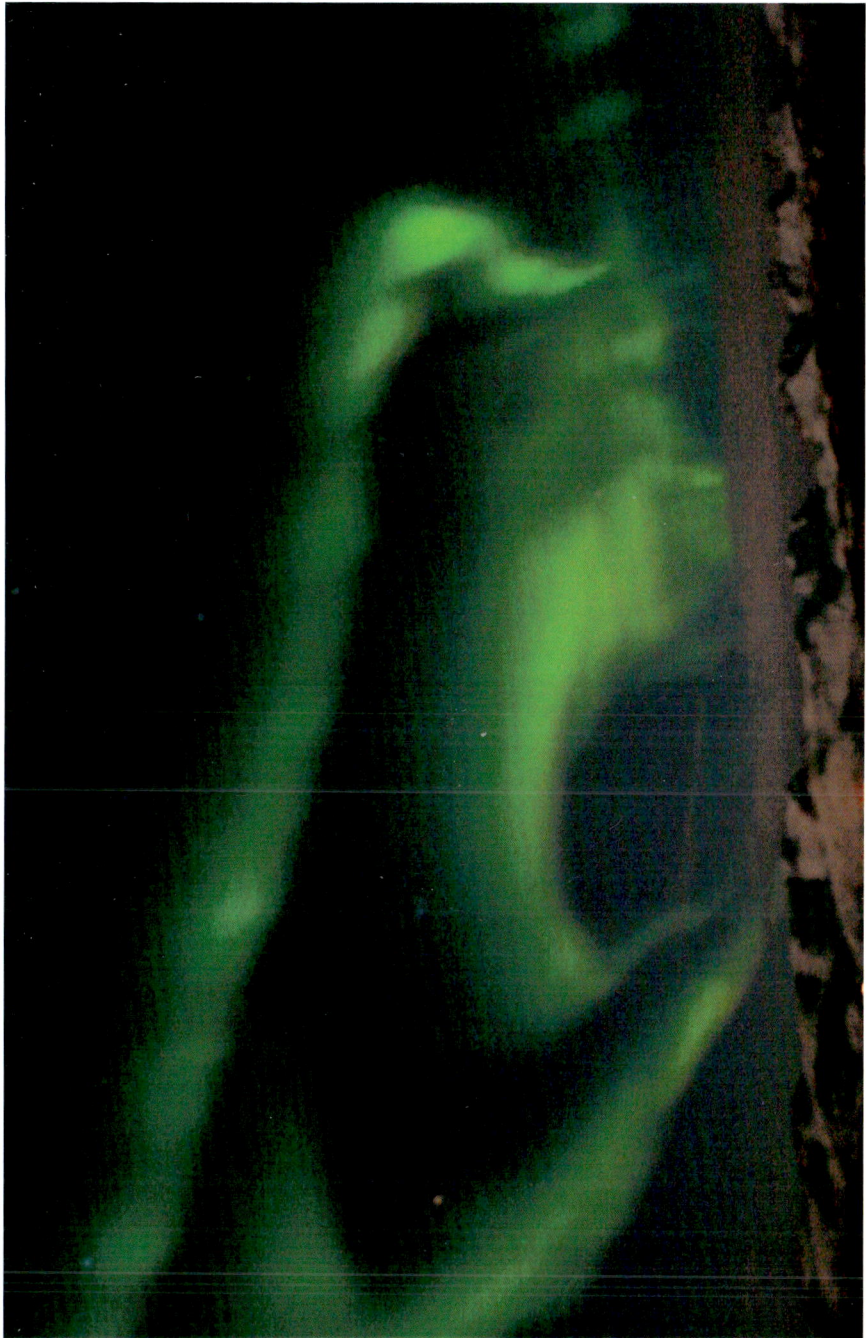

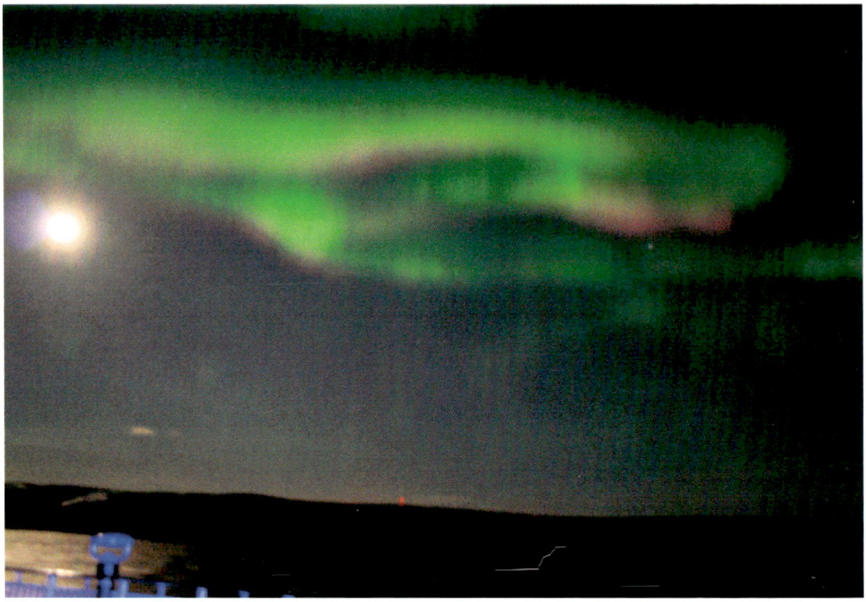

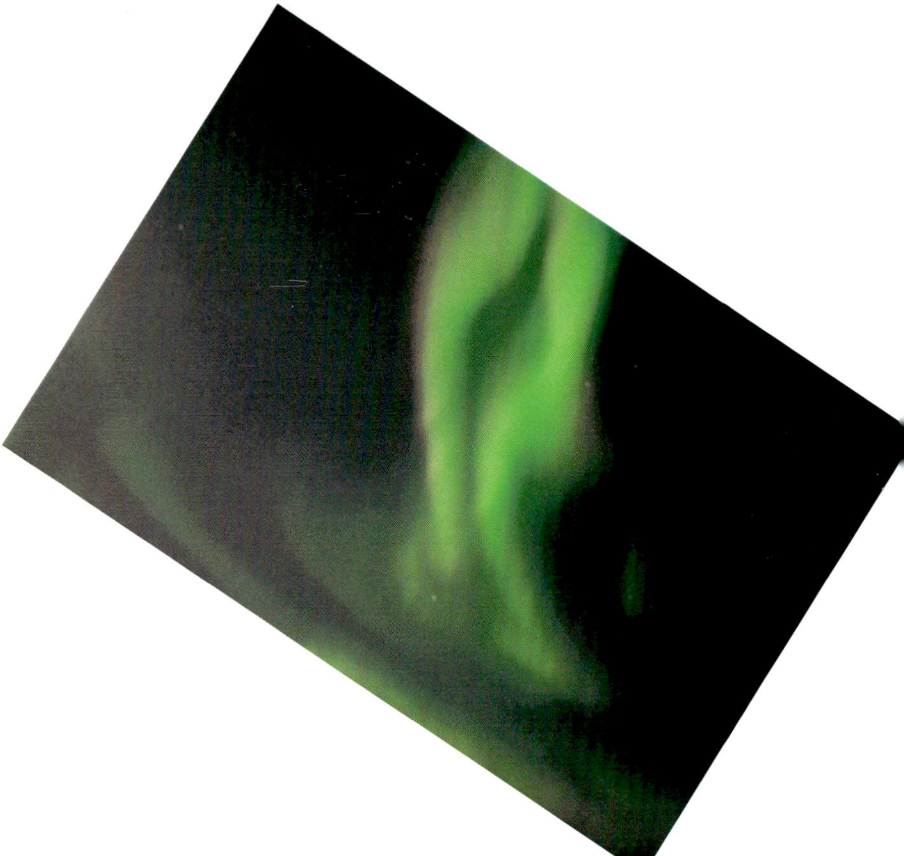

'The Deck of Cards', Texas T Tyler.

'Ave Maria' so popular, there are many versions.

'Hear the Word of The Lord' (Them bones, them dry bones), Ezekiel

Spirituals, very popular, especially 'Swing Low, Sweet Chariot'.

'The Lord's Prayer' needing no comment.

'Put your hand in the hand'.

'Delilah', made famous by Tom Jones.

'Turn Turn Turn'.

King David Oratorio.

Gospel Psalms.

'How are the Mighty Fallen'.

'Hallelujah' by Leonard Cohen. Six verses of the story of King David – the Biblical King. He spent five years writing it, in a Buddhist Retreat, commenting later, 'Stick with it long enough and it will yield' – in other words, never give up.

'The only way is out', Cliff Richard.

'Spirit in the Sky'; there are many different recordings of this hit.

'Shadrach, Meshach, and Abednego', 1962 song revived from the '30s. The story is from the 1st Book of Daniel telling how 'they were saved by God', from the fiery furnace.

'A day at a Time, Sweet Jesus', another big hit.

'The Preacher Man' (Eccles 1 1-11).

'My Brother's Keeper', Music Film.

'At the time of the going down of the sun' Josh 10-87 and Chron 2 18-34

Bob Marley kept a Bible near, not only because it proved a limitless source of inspiration for lyric writing, but also for help and wisdom.

It is true that 'music' lifts spirits and helps with morale, referring here again particularly to the First World War. In that war, often referred to as 'The Great War', Regimental Bands were essential, and not only for their stirring, popular sound, but with words to match. The thinking behind hearing this music was also to 'engender home sickness', intentional, to have the soldiers think about home and what was happening in the war, therefore encouraging them to be determined to 'soldier' on, no matter what!

John Tavener, composer, who died early this year, hailed as one of the 'very best creative talents', said his inspiration was from the Bible. His music included the whole of the story of Jonah, set to music, St. John of the Cross, The Protecting Veil, and The Song for Athene, chosen to be played at the funeral of Diana, Princess of Wales, in 1997.

His music reflected the spiritual side of his nature, but he was also one of the 'trend setters' in modern life. With flamboyant dress, and long hair, he was one of the party people. Apparently, he was a 'one-off', and one who was, at the same time deeply religious. Someone asked, 'Was it religion or spirituality that spurred his work?' 'When I am writing, I feel I am in contact with God,' continuing, 'How intolerable to be not in contact with God.'

His music was 'for our time', influenced as it was by different cultures, languages, religions, spirituality. He wrote devotional works for the concert hall as well as the church, seeming to have a strong intuition to write what people are 'needing'.

He had a strong intuition to write 'what people need! Was it religion or 'spirituality' that spurred his work...?

'Religion/religious', is 'believing in a religion', and carrying out its practices. To be spiritual is 'to care'.

This is the 'New Age' we are now living in; The Age of Aquarius, where the changes forecast centuries ago are gradually taking place. The spiritual revolution forecast is now in evidence, in which there will be a 'coming together', a caring and sharing as never seen before. The Pope has called for a coming together of all faiths, in prayer, for our world – so grave are the crises we are all facing.

The forecast – there will be a great burst of human potential, physical, intellectual and spiritual – is happening. The development of resources we never knew we had is happening.

The evolution of a spiritual awakening is the foundation of a Basic Christian Community; groups are slowly growing into 'Neighbourhood Christian Communities', sharing together, relating to others at a deeper than usual level, sharing their spiritual experiences; happening now.

• • •

Allan MacDonald writes, in *A Path Prepared*, 'We realise the tremendous task we undertake to try to bring before a material world something that is everyone's birth right'!

Something that is our birth right! Our spirituality in competition with our material world! (Spiritual beings in a physical body, living in a material world!)

Thinking seriously about it though, is it *really* so difficult for spirituality and materialism to coexist harmoniously together? Are there *really* so many obstacles to overcome the gap between the two… or am *I* missing the point?

Why is the media so obsessed with giving us sad, bad, horrible news stories? Is it because they are the ones that sell papers? Or have we been 'brainwashed', saturated with them over the years; inured, unable to expect anything different? Sad, bad, horrible news has always been around; but now, with new technology, we get everything from everywhere, with no punches pulled. Can we not have a day once in a while, of 'good, happy, decent 'news'; a day when we gradually bring in the 'higher' side of life? It does exist! We are becoming more attuned to the spirit world, through a new understanding of its message (however that new understanding, 'awakening', comes about, whether it be through a profound revelation, a coincidence, a dream, an experience, an 'angel', or whatever). We begin to *see*, to *feel* an influence of a spiritual nature in our lives that has always 'been', and 'is', and will always 'be'; we cannot exist without it because we *are* spirit, here and now.

('It is the spirit that gives life.'[11])

We are that indefinable energy that *is* spirit. We are ever partakers of the 'love' and 'care' we can always rely on, 'no matter where we go or what we do'; and to call upon, by that 'special' name, you or I can relate to: The Universal Energy; The Life Force; The Creator; the 'Unnamed Something'; Father God.

We may not go to church, or go to church regularly, but we know about 'prayer', and the power thereof. Hands up who has not, at some time in their lives, asked for its help?

'More things are wrought by prayer than this world dreams of.'[12]

We understand the power of 'feelings' and the major part they play in our lives; intuition, conscience, angels – talked about and accepted as never before; it seems that most of us believe in angels (something good in everything we see – a good philosophy). Kindness, caring and sharing are strongly in evidence in our world today, with more of us giving to charity and offering our services to help wherever we can. Are all these things not evidence of 'spirituality' thriving, in this our 'material world'? There is a new, stronger understanding of our planet and that we 'share' it with *all* life, the animal kingdom (our brothers and sisters), as St. Francis beautifully expressed in the thirteenth century. We buy free-range eggs – yes, perhaps because we know they will be good for us; of a much better quality than the ones from poor birds cooped up so tightly that they can't move, and frustrated to the point of attacking each other. We also buy free-range eggs, because we now 'understand', and 'feel' for the dreadful life of the poor caged chickens. (Fish can feel pain...)

• • •

We may not yet know it, but we are, all of us, well on the way to putting 'spiritual', with a capital 'S', into our lives. It is on the agenda! Of course' there is a spiritual revolution – it's happening now, all the time, as you read these words; a slow, steady, positive expression, in different ways to maybe thirty years ago, but it is there; an expression of our care, concern, love, and, what is also most important, of our *understanding*—

If we are 'tuned in', with understanding, and with love and sincerity in our hearts, we know that to receive a communication from the other side of life (the spirit world), however seemingly small or insignificant it may seem, is priceless. Today, in the New Age we are now in, millions of us understand and are part of the 'team' helping to bring the Two Worlds together; accepting the truth that we are spirit here and now (we live to live), and to 'die' is simply to 'shed', to shake off, this 'top coat', this 'over coat', this body of ours... Is it as if we always knew anyway, but somehow, the world, changing as it is, is now a world where we can experience *and discuss* such things – openly?

> The Bible tells us: They have eyes but they see not,
> ears but they hear not. Ps 135 v16 – 17

Those words were perhaps true in centuries past, but the evidence is not so true today.

Today, for the most part, we are 'believers'. We 'see', we 'hear', and we also understand the 'deeper' meaning of the above words from the Bible; how we live; how we love; how we care (in other words, to be 'spiritual').

• • •

This chapter, before ending, has three remarkable 'evidences' of 'spirit' to report, touching lives in three different ways; the first one heartfelt, positive and with hope; the second amusing and enough evidence to start a whole crowd 'buzzing'; the third, well you will see, and judge for yourselves. Please read on.

Anita, who told us about her grandfather being a changed man after his visit to the spirit world, where he was 'warned' what would happen to him if he didn't change his ways, gives us a moving account of a vision she had days after her husband's passing, before his funeral.

Devastated by his death (even though she is a true believer in an afterlife), she was due to visit the chapel of rest in the morning, with her son Ian; she awoke at 6 a.m. and could not get back to sleep. She lay for more than an hour, trying to focus on the music they had chosen to be played after the service, while they were leaving the crematorium. Not knowing how it happened, she must have fallen into a deep sleep, which in turn, became a vision. Here are Anita's own words of her experience.

'As if in a dream, I was being taken to a derelict building with concrete blocks patched together with cement, and broken windows which had been boarded up. The man with me was the undertaker, but he was very casually dressed in grey trousers, grey shirt and a grey zipped-up cardigan. As we walked past this derelict building (there was also a roller-shutter garage door), we began to reach the new chapel of rest, which was behind the derelict building – that had been the old one.

'The next thing I remember was being in a small room with two windows and three beds, just like a hospital ward. I said to the undertaker, "My husband isn't in here, my husband will be in a coffin." He pointed to the third bed under the left-hand window and he said, "There's your husband over there."

'When I looked over to the bed, you were sitting up and wearing the pyjamas you had on the night you left me (passed away). Your auburn hair was very curly on your forehead, and there were tight baby curls on the side of your head. Everything was in colour, and as I looked at you, a stronger ray of light shone over you making the colours look stronger. You looked so young and handsome, just like you looked when we got married. As I moved towards you, I said, "Oh John, look at your hair." You said, "I'm OK, I love you," and you were gone. I turned to the man (the undertaker) and said, "That was wonderful, how did you do that?" He said, "We have ways," and I said, "But you even had my husband's voice." He replied, "That's because it *is* your husband." The next thing I remember is that it was 9 a.m. and I awoke in tears and went downstairs to tell Ian what had happened.

'I had never been to the chapel of rest previously, and when Ian and I went later in the day, it was exactly as I had seen it in the vision. The derelict building, broken windows, cemented breezeblocks, and the roller shutter garage door; walking past it all, to the new chapel of rest, there was my husband laid out in a small room with two windows; his head was where his bed had been (in my vision), with his feet at the right side, under the other window.'

(It is believed that to have an 'experience' or to 'see', in colour, is very spiritual.)

• • •

Steve's father, Bob, who passed away some twenty years ago, was a mechanic, serving his apprenticeship for two years. Later, he joined the air force as a mechanic, and served for a number of years. Finally, he joined the police force. Always well liked and 'true', a pillar of the community, it was a very popular decision, many years later, when he was made a police superintendent.

At his funeral, besides the family and crowds who had gathered to show their respect for such a good man, was a guard of honour. Police officers, in full uniform, lined the way, proud to be there, also to show their respect for Bob – a 'would-be' friend to all.

Everything proceeded correctly, all in place, no 'hitches' in evidence at this very 'smart', well attended funeral, when, just as the hearse began to turn a very slight bend in the road, to arrive at the front door of the crematorium, somehow, and just about everyone noticed, one brake light went off.

After the service and 'commiserations', the 'sad' occasion turned to one of laughter and real amusement, as the state of the 'faulty' brake light was discussed, poured over, and the decision made, it had to be Bob! It *had* to be Bob! Correct and exact as he was, in all things, he was now presiding over his own funeral; being sure that remembrance of his years, his happy years as a mechanic 'were not forgotten'. Evidence for all to see, and evidence accepted.

• • •

Think of how, in this new century of ours, we have changed, or are gradually changing our position on religion – going to church, or not going to church; and are we still of a mind to say our prayers, 'think spiritual', act with the good of others in mind, or are we really all 'self'? Have you heard of the poem, 'Footprints in the Sand'? These are the words of someone in a desperately sad situation, with no one to turn to, asking 'where was God' when needed.

'I noticed that at many times along the path of my life, especially at the very lowest and saddest times, there was only one set of footprints in the sand.'

Heidi is someone who has a very demanding and responsible job, does not go to church, but still has her prayer book and Bible tucked away somewhere, and would not part with them. She takes comfort from carrying items such as a rosary that hangs by her bed, and when in stressful times, carries it with her, and she always gathers strength from having it there (knowing it is always there when needed). She says she doesn't 'pray', but when troubled, sends out 'thoughts', and feels they are answered (prayers!). Heidi is also someone who loves a night out at the pub. She loves playing darts, and sport, and now bravely tells us why she had the last verse of 'Footprints in the Sand' tattooed on her arm, from elbow to wrist.

Here are her own words on how she coped with the hard times that we all come across at some point in our lives.

'My tattoo is the last verse of the footprint poem. "The Lord replied, my precious child, I love you and will never leave you. During times of suffering when you only see one set of footprints in the sand, it was then that I carried you."

'I remember reading that poem when I was much younger, mother being quite religious and it's stuck with me over the years.

'My reason for getting the last verse inked onto my arm was pretty much for two reasons.

The first one is that it represents my values in life: trust, loyalty and integrity (doing the right thing, supporting each other).

'The second reason was to show my values to Billy [Heidi's husband] when he was diagnosed with cancer three years ago. It was important to me to get this tattoo done prior to any treatment he received, as I knew it would be a tough time for us. We got through it and so far, all is going well, long may it continue!

'We also renewed our wedding vows one year later as a sign of a fresh start.'

Perhaps quoting the words from the Bible, 'Man shall not live by bread alone', at the beginning of this chapter does not fall on deaf ears after all.

Anthony Trevor was a natural psychic. From the age of seven years, he could see spirit people, and throughout his long life he accepted that he could see things that a lot of other people couldn't; he could see the spirit world almost everywhere, but on one occasion he was 'flabbergasted', as he said at the time. He was standing at the bar of the Bull and Bush in Hampstead Heath, London, when a man dressed as a highwayman rushed in. The figure strode to the bar and banged on the counter with his fist, and of course, the barman, who couldn't see him anyway, ignored him, so the stranger grabbed his pistol, shot at the barman and disappeared!

Chapter Six

Colour My World

> *'This have I found, saith the Preacher'*, Eccles 7 – 27
> *'Time and chance happen to all, rich and poor alike'*, Eccles 9 – 2

A SMALL NUMBER OF people took part in a survey for me on the above title, 'Colour my World'. They did not have any clues as to the meaning of it, and answers could be as long or as short as they chose – one word would be fine. Would *you* like to 'have a go' at this, before reading the chapter, you could write your answer – remember one word would be enough, at the back of the book. (Go on, have a go, what colours *your* world?)

• • •

February 2015

Katie, a twenty-one year old beautician from the Northeast, was so moved by the sad story and pictures in the newspaper, of sixty-seven-year-old Alan. Alan was so vulnerable – disabled, born with sight and growth problems – that she felt she had to do *something* to help him in his hour of need, and immediately launched an appeal to raise money for him (putting it out to the universe?), by way of an online donation page. She had never done anything like that before and hoped to raise maybe a figure of £500.00. Within days, the figure had reached a quarter of a million and was still rising, with donations coming in from all over the world.

Alan was attacked for money by a stranger outside his own home, money that he did not have anyway; he was knocked down, and suffered a broken collarbone, leaving him too scared ever to return home. A committed Christian, Alan has said that 'he always knew there were a lot of good people in the world', but how amazed he is at what has happened since the attack! The money keeps going up and up, and meeting Katie, who will be a friend for life, was 'just magical'.

Is it 'magical'… is it chance, or a result of 'consequences' that must themselves have evolved from 'chance'…or is it coincidence? Remember that a coincidence is God's way of working a miracle anonymously – therefore, Alan is right, it must be magical. God's magic.

When Alan opened his front door to go outside and move the rubbish bin that Sunday evening, to be ready for collection the next day, he did not know that he was setting in motion actions that would change his life forever.

When Katie read the article about Alan in the paper and saw the picture, she did not know that her strong feelings, her 'inner' hurt, for a complete stranger, someone in distress, would take her on a new pathway in life, a different journey, where some day, later, looking back at it all, she might say, 'Well I never… amazing!'

It's interesting to note that the press, local and national, gave good news coverage to this story, and it was even remarked on at the press preview that night that the 'press were covering a "good" news story', as if it were something unusual. Well I never!

'Colour our world.' To understand that our every action, every word, every thought, sets in motion something that will have repercussions somewhere in our universe is awesome. And so, here we are again, thinking about 'energies', 'vibrations', 'The Interconnected Universe'.[1] 'Human beings and all living things, a coalescence of energy in a field of energy connected to every other thing in the world.'[2] (It is a jolt for us as we realise just *how* responsible we are for our thoughts and actions.)

Our personal world is affected, coloured, by *everything* we see or hear, or interact with; our emotions 'buzzing' with events, interests, big and small; our mood, happy, sad, irritated, amused. We are affected by everything that happens in our lives, every incident, and colour is often used in the vocabulary itself, for example, clear as black and white; as white as chalk, green fingers, seeing red; a red letter day, tickled pink, that old blue feeling, a golden year, a black mood. Of course, we realise, you and I, that the words 'colour my world' go far, far, deeper than any symbolization with 'colour'.

Life is *the* great adventure for all of us, whether young or old, rich or poor, fit and well, not so fit or well. As someone recently remarked, 'How extraordinary ordinary life is, and the way we learn from each other.' This reminds me of the old Arabic saying, 'nothing is certain, and everything is possible'; and that we should be 'believing' enough (remembering that we are spiritual beings in a physical body), have faith enough, not to fret or worry – as we all do at times – whatever the problem. Have you noticed how often we marvel at the way things work out? The problems, the worries, the disappointments, that are at times apparently unsolvable, 'impossible', but with the right attitude, and sending out of thoughts/prayers, there can be a complete turnaround.

Have you ever had something so serious, a life-changing experience, happen to you that you really did not want to happen? You begged, you prayed, in your deep 'inner moments', that whatever it was would not come about, but it did. It then seemed that your life, and the rest of your life, would be shrouded, clouded in darkness. Then, suddenly, 'out of the blue', things changed, lifted, often in an 'impossible to imagine', unpredictable, 'magical' – that word again – way. It changed to become the Best Thing that had ever happened to you (and to me; a long time ago). This has been the story of the whole of the human race, since the beginning.

'Nothing new under the sun.'

'Time and chance happen to all, rich and poor alike,' saith the preacher man.

We all dream, at one time or another; some of us are regular dreamers, enjoying the state of complete relaxation found in a good night's sleep with the recollection (if we do remember) of having a pleasant experience during the sleep state. There are those who have no recollection at all of dreaming, and so do not believe that they dream; and there are others, who, according to the depth and reality of the dream experience, can perhaps class it as having had a 'vision'. We all understand the unpleasantness of having a nightmare, being only-too pleased to wake up and get out of it, put it out of mind as soon as possible; and then there is dreaming in colour.

Dreaming in colour; I wonder, is it an unusual experience, and could it be linked with the spiritual? To have an out of body experience in colour is, we are told, very spiritual. Jane always dreams in colour. Her dreams are vivid – and 'real'. Could she be having an out of body experience within the dream state? One dream she experienced years ago as a recurring dream. She was always out in beautiful countryside and there was always a hill, but the peculiarity was the profusion of *blue apples*. Beautiful blue, shiny apples, which she chased after and collected in amazement and joy – even to running up the hill in pursuit of them… always chasing and collecting blue apples.

In The *Quantum Dream Dictionary*,[3] spiritually, an apple suggests a new beginning and a freshness of approach, while the colour blue, which is the prime healing colour, suggests relaxation, sleep and peacefulness.

Thinking about it, 'what colours *your* world? Recently, as I mentioned at the beginning of this chapter, I conducted a small survey among friends and strangers alike, asking them the same question. I asked them – without giving any hint or clue as to what I meant by it (the question), to answer in one word, or two, or a sentence or two, or a paragraph; to answer in any way they wanted, 'What colours your world?' and I was surprised at how interested and keen most people were to take part. Why don't you join in? Write your answer at the back of the book, date it, then you will have something to look back on, and compare.

To continue with this theme (colour my world), one of the great joys of life is to have a good laugh, and when we do, the memory seems to stay with us forever.

'A cheerful heart is good medicine.' Prov 17 – 22

There is an old German saying that if we don't have a good laugh at least once a day, it is a day wasted; while the simple words of a Victorian headmistress, 'We all do our best when we are happy,' surely ring true.

'A cheerful heart is good medicine.' The Bible tells us so. How many times have we felt uplifted, released, freed, even if only for a short time, from some form of worry, stress, heartache, by an unexpected, good, hearty, 'old-fashioned', belly laugh, enough to bring tears to the eyes. It is true, we all feel better after a good laugh, and we are advised that, for our well-being, we should get into the habit of keeping a smile on our face. Imagine if we all did that, all of us walking around the supermarket with a permanent grin...but smiling, as does exercise, releases endorphins from the brain into the blood stream, helping to give us that feel-good factor.

Have you noticed how talking to certain people can give you a happy, uplifted feeling? Is it what they say, or how they say it, or both? It is called being positive; while the opposite is true of a forever downbeat grumbler, complainer, with nothing much to say that is not negative. Have you noticed that if we try to see the funny side of things (there are people who are naturally sunny and good at this – always looking on the bright side of life), we can usually find a few amusing, even laughable, incidents, happening around us nearly every day, that can be turned into a good laugh. I suppose it is having the right attitude, and thinking positively in response to the question, 'Is the glass half empty or half full?' Whatever the situation, or problem, if at all possible, then is the time for you, and for me, to reply positively, answering the question, shouting the answer out to the universe, 'It is half full!' Yes!!! (With three exclamation marks.)

I am sure we will, all of us, have experienced the fun, the 'love', the 'enjoyment', to be had from nature, the animal world, and all God's creatures, great and small. (Think here of a kitten with a ball of wool; a tiny bird struggling, determined to get a long twig into the opening of a small birdhouse, moving it this way and that, even upside down…high hopes.) You will have your own stories and memories of wonderful times with your pets, colouring your life as maybe nothing else ever can. In simply observing the turn of the seasons there is joy; the budding of new growth into colours artists have tried forever to copy; and with colours and patterns designers know they are always on to 'a winner'; all part of the bounteous, limitless, flow and ebb, ebb and flow of our beautiful world.

• • •

A newspaper headline, 'A November Spectacle of Magic and Mystery', presents us with an outstanding series of photographs of thousands of starlings starting their murmuration as dusk falls, on the English/Scottish border, the reason for this spectacle not definitely known. In spectacular pictures, from an Arctic wildlife refuge,[4] with the heading, 'I got rhythm – animals like to dance', we see polar bears trying to balance in shallow water by the sea, in time to a beat. Monkeys, apes, birds and even sea lions, all have the ability to move in time to a musical beat; a chance discovery (was it really chance?), in 2008, by neuroscientists, showed even cockatoos have rhythm, when they saw a video of a pet cockatoo called Snowball dancing to music by the Backstreet Boys. The daughter of the family, noticing how it bobbed its head in time to the music, began dancing with it, teaching it to move its feet. One professor of psychology said he had never seen anything like it.

A polar bear standing on its hind legs, waving back to a cameraman completely spontaneously is so funny, always good for a laugh, or a smile, at least; animals, birds, even the trees – do they sway in time to a special beat, the rhythm of the 'universe', possibly they do? Animals and birds obviously know how good dancing is for you, and me! Come on, put that disc on, and let's have a good jive. New, at the time, twenties' dance music (the Charleston for one) was frowned on and banned by the establishment, until it was proved to be, and accepted as a form of exercise. How far we have come in our world, and yet apparently we can still prove (if we were historians/antiquarians, or scientists), if we go in to all the innovations deeply enough, there really is nothing new under the sun; dancing is only one of the countless pleasures we enjoy, and have enjoyed since the beginning – of everything.

The facts are that life has answers built into it, and *nature* has already solved all our problems.[5] Science already knows that animals use organised sound patterns to communicate with each other in a system similar to human language. The unbelievable made real is a 'whale that learnt to talk'; and science is now set to bring about communication with animals, even to detect the fleeting thoughts of fish. (Fish can feel pain.)

So many of us are familiar with the 'language of silence' with regard to our brothers and sisters in the natural world, yet how many times have we said, 'There is no such thing as a dumb animal.' Colouring our world, our lives, as they do, animals speak to our hearts, touch our hearts, and to hear a moving story of interaction between animal and human is surely as good for us as is the sister emotion, laughter.

> He had worked at the zoo for many years, with the giraffes, and now, absent through illness, and knowing he was coming to the end of his life, he asked to be taken back to see them, and to say goodbye. Other keepers, watching, could hardly contain their emotion and wonder at the sensitivity shown by the animals to this man; closing in around him, their every movement, every action, portraying in the language of silence their delight in seeing him again. Yet it was so obvious

that their delight was tinged with sadness, as they understood, and accepted that this was his goodbye.

A kitten found itself in a bear compound, with a bear that looked after it, and it refused to leave. The love and friendship they had found in each other's company was noticed by all; a source of amusement and disbelief at first that soon became one of deep respect.

Snails, very sociable, hibernate together, and have a homing device to keep within their community. Whatever happened to one the other day, reported to me as seen making its way, and already halfway up, a telegraph pole, is anyone's guess!

There is harmony in function in all natural life. In all nature, plants, trees, animals, birds, insects 'blend in', send 'messages' about where to meet to other members of the species, and not just about mating... . We see a sense of love and caring shine through – birds circling, wheeling round and round distressed at the predicament of another; a seagull flying backwards and forwards at the edge of the sea, fearful for its partner, not able to move, bobbing helplessly with the flow of the water. We see it everywhere, when we learn to notice – in all nature, as it is in human kind.

'If I collapse, a nudge from a little wet nose can save me.' This is a headline drawing our attention to the terrifying condition known as narcolepsy, sudden unconsciousness, now finding help from a surprising source, the animal world. Dogs and other animals/birds, can be trained to be alert to the needs of sufferers (in various illnesses), and can rouse them, bring them round from an unconscious state. Tricia, a sufferer, one of apparently 30,000 in the UK, is so grateful to have Dusty, her miniature poodle, to protect her. Dusty knows exactly when she has an attack, being able to tune in to Tricia's condition; he suddenly leaps to his feet, barks, and begins pawing her, and burrowing into her armpit with his nose. This is enough to bring Tricia round. Cocoa the cat woke Jane up twice in the night when her sugar levels were very low; so having Cocoa is not only a great source of comfort and pleasure and love, 'colouring her world as nothing else could', but also her life-saver.

On a busy Saturday in December 2014, in Kanpur, India, crowds of people were astonished to witness the sight of a monkey save the life of another monkey, who fell unconscious, after being electrocuted by a railway track...saved by the quick thinking and action of another.

Stories of our brothers and sisters in the animal kingdom come from everywhere; and here is this final, special one, showing the intelligence and feelings of a tiny Yorkshire terrier, *and* with a postscript at the end, offering proof that animals do survive death.

Jamie, ever shaggy, with beautiful thick, blue-black hair and huge saucer-brown eyes, was a little darling, stepping out in life fearlessly, like the true soldier that he was. He was happy, content, and seemingly not disturbed by anyone or anything, except that he did not like birds, and especially the ones that appeared daily in his garden (maybe because they were always so well fed and watered). He was unbelievably jealous of these birds, as you will see in the following incident.

Jamie belonged to close friends of mine, and one day, a few of us were sitting in the back garden enjoying the late afternoon summer sun. My friend's mother put out some biggish pieces of home-made cake for the birds, then she joined us for a chat; her husband was inside the house reading the paper. We noticed how Jamie stood and stared while the cake was being thrown on the ground, and how he then sat down, still staring at it, obviously deep in thought. Time passed, and although we had watched him, finally moving, going in and out of the house, nothing special was thought of it until my friend's father appeared, asking, 'What's going on here?' As he was reading his paper, he was also aware of Jamie coming and going. It was not until, finally, curious about just what he was doing, he looked down at his feet to where all the action seemed to be taking place, to find, a pile of cake crumbs and just in time to see Jamie appear again with yet more.

You can imagine the laughter and the amazement as we marvelled at the thinking behind the behaviour of the little dog. Jamie had been sitting there working out what he could do to prevent the birds getting the cake. Thinking, 'I can't eat it all, I can't sit here guarding it all day,' he'd decided his best bet was to transport it into the house – which he did successfully!

It was so sad; a dreadful hurt for family and friends alike when Jamie died unexpectedly at the age of seven years from a heart problem. However, the grief was lightened considerably when, within days of his passing, news came of his 'return'.

Peter, the son-in-law of the family, was working in the Middle East at the time. Shocked, feeling bad on hearing about the loss of the 'little fella', as he called him, he was trying to settle down for the night; as he turned to lean on his elbow, looking for a more comfortable position, he saw two huge eyes staring up at him from the bottom of the bed. Then, he saw a whirlwind of shaggy hair hurtling towards him, only to disappear as quickly as it had appeared; the vision of Jamie, the little dog, evaporating into thin air, leaving all as if it had never been.

The question was often asked, by those who heard the story, 'Why did Jamie, make his appearance far away from home, where comfort was needed?' It took a long time for those involved to understand that love is the greatest motivator of all... . True, unselfish love; Jamie, in his new state, understood, more than anyone, where was the greatest need, and no doubt, used this chance, 'his new energy', to go there. Whatever and however, the experience (they soon heard about it) was the best uplift anyone could ever have, the family realising that, through their sorrow, came the indisputable proof of 'survival'; priceless evidence, come about in a most extraordinary way.

• • •

Colour, as are music and the arts, is the language of the soul. Let's think of the link between emotions and colours – the colour red for example, stands for anger, stimulation, excitement; green for peace, calm, balance and a connection with nature (green also associated with envy); thinking about it in this way, perhaps we understand more fully, the link between colour and our feelings, emotions, moods. Colour healing, which dates back thousands of years, is a holistic therapy, treating the whole of the person, bringing forward the 'inner self', the spirit, the real you, the real me. You will know, better than anyone, the colour or colours that suit you; for fashion, decorating your home, and for all the personal items you carry with you in life. In life, we are surrounded by colour everywhere, and we know that the inner, personal expression of ourselves can also be perceived by the choices we make.

A top business executive uses music to help him with his work. If, when going to an important meeting, he needs to be tough, he listens to suitable music to put him in the right mood; the same with meetings that will be more quiet, reflective, thoughtful. Always he relies on music to prepare him, and so it is to his inner self through music that he turns for the advice and support he needs.

Frazer, a young man who claims that he was 'saved from the streets' by music, tells how he was brought up the hard way in north London. Finding work was not easy, and there were too many temptations around, and he admits that he was no angel. Then, finding his talent as a singer, a one-man band, playing the keyboards, drums, and writing and producing all his own music, he says, 'Thank God people supported my music.' He is hoping for success with his debut solo single record, 'Killer', out now. Whatever the outcome, it seems that he has not only found his talent, but a new, solid enthusiasm for life with his wonderful gift; *and* he has found an inner strength that will carry him forward and see him through the rough patches we all go through from time to time.

Guy was a talented viola player in the thirties, at the time of the great depression. With no work, or even any prospect of work, and with a young family to feed, his own sense of despair led to his own depression, and to a pawn shop, where he handed in his precious viola, and took out a pistol to shoot himself. Walking, thinking, he passed a concert hall giving a free concert, and the music was The New World Symphony. Guy slipped into the hall, intending to listen, then go to the toilet at the back, to do the deed, take his own life. Becoming so wrapped up in the music – it talked to him, speaking in such 'exhilarating language' – by the last movement, he was uplifted, strengthened, and ready to get out there and have another go at finding work…which he found, and has since always said, 'Music saved my life.' (Coloured his world, and saved his life.)

Art itself has moved into new areas of creativity, with the intention of encouraging us to think seriously about what we see and experience in our visits to art centres and galleries, hoping that we might be persuaded to have a go ourselves. All these things (as mentioned previously in this book) are happening in music, dance, drama, 'life'; finding our inner selves. A new craze creeping in (great for releasing stress) is colouring books for adults. Artists are now employed to create colouring books designed especially for adults, and they have really caught on with the public, as the owner of a new craft shop has told me, new stock of the books selling out within days.

What is it all about? This new age of ours encourages us to be creative, to think more deeply about things we may have just skimmed over in the past; maybe to find our hidden talents (we all have them), and use them to take us in a new, more interesting, fulfilling direction; nourishment, music for our inner self, our spirit. It's good to think 'high, good, beautiful thoughts', attracting yet more high, good, beautiful thoughts, lifting us ever higher; now well-tuned in to the spiritual, our 'higher self'. Poetry; be inspired, write your own words, why not? Words of love, friendship, caring, encouragement may all be coming through our newly awakened inner selves. Magic (that word again) is coming into us, flying in to us – our legacy, yes, our newly awakened legacy, our spirit, and all a product of the New Age…while we still await the prophesy of a prophet, a messiah, a teacher, yet to come.

• • •

During the time of the First World War, 1914-1918, the army, based in Gallipoli, was saved from death by thirst, through the skill, knowledge and art of a water-diviner, sometimes known as a dowser; the water-diviner, using his skill with forked sticks, rods or a pendulum, to source water held below the ground. 'This ability is as common as musical, or other forms of "genius".'[6] Think of it, a whole army saved by the gift, the skill, knowledge, of a water-diviner. This story now takes us back in the direction of 'energies'.

Energy, energies; remember the amazing skill of Uri Geller, famous for his spoon bending, and who has gone on to use his knowledge in much deeper, serious ways, helping governments and other bodies to understand, accept, and use the untapped forces around us, including of course the power of thought to make the world a better, safer, place.

Energy is in and around us everywhere, in all living things; the trees, the sky, the rocks, sand and sea, everywhere; as the song says (but not referring to energy), 'in every breath we take, in every move we make', energy. And as we realise the benefits we can all gain from recognising who we *really* are; spirit, in a physical body, opening the door to these untapped energies around us, the 'life force', the 'universal energy'; becoming aware of our own – yes, you and me, untapped potential; life suddenly becomes thrilling, exciting, nothing to be afraid of. Full of amazing possibilities!

Ted worked hard all day selling pancakes, sweet and salty, outside a hall where a crystal fair was in full swing (crystals and alternate therapies). The scores of people, coming and going, fascinated him, as he too was kept busy, the visitors stopping off for a pancake or two at his stall. 'But what was the crystal fair all about?' he wondered, to attract so many people of all ages. He did know something about the power of crystals. He knew that the first radio was a 'crystal set', and he remembered hearing something about early aeroplanes and crystals.

The busy day finally ended as successfully as it had begun, a few reluctant-to-leave stragglers, the last count of what might prove to be a record-breaking day, with Ruth, the organiser, highly delighted. Ted looked in after he had dismantled his stall and packed away the equipment, while Ruth, although still busy, signalled to him to stay and have a chat. Together, they viewed the last of what had been a huge, beautiful display of crystals. Ted, at last getting his wish to know more, was treated to a mini-explanation about a few of the stones. 'The power of crystals lies in their ability to hold and transmit energy. Crystal energy can help with healing; focusing our minds on what we want to do, achieve.' Ted was interested enough to want to buy one for his father, and thoroughly enjoyed picking up one, then another, holding each one in turn, as Ruth suggested, until suddenly he gave a shout, 'Oh dear, what's happening?' as he felt a surge of energy sweep through his body. He ended up choosing one for his father, a few more for other people, and no doubt picked up one for himself.

November 2012: Queensland, Australia, celebrated the total eclipse of the sun by the moon, one of nature's greatest phenomena. Tens of thousands gathered to witness this event; however, clouds threatened to spoil the party – but they didn't; the clouds cleared, and the crowds and crowds of people were given a perfect view of totality – the amazing moment when the moon completely covers the sun, and a faint halo appears. Wonderful as it is, to witness such a sight, the truly Greatest Show on Earth (but in the heavens, if you know what I mean), Award must go to The Northern Lights in all their glory – or to give them their proper name, the *Aurora Borealis*.

What a name and what a show! And as they appear, often slowly, hesitantly at first (are there sounds of an orchestra in accompaniment?), to see, the unbelievably vibrant colours careering on finally into patterns; crossing, sweeping, crisscrossing, creating glittering spaces and shapes never seen before – over the whole sky – wondrous patterns, super-human patterns, woven as they go. Heads swivelling this way and that, not to miss anything; lighter and darker shades of every colour, dotted with a sparkling of silver, moving, swirling at great speed; changing, forming yet new patterns as quickly as the old ones have come into being.... . The excitement, the scene, the lights perform as if trying to better themselves in answer to the delight of the crowds, now reduced to tears. There are tears falling everywhere; people crying, hugging each other, friends and strangers alike. *We were all one*, on the four nights that we were privileged to witness this spectacle.

We were all one, clapping, cheering, shouting, the 'oohs and ahs' in unison, never before more sincerely or emotionally expressed. The whole of the night sky was dancing and shimmying to the rhythm of the stars. The sky was the stage, the whole world the audience. This was truly heaven being witnessed on earth – in every sense of the word.[7]

• • •

Harold Sharp, a well-known and well-loved, medium, healer, writer, philosopher, was a troubled man. Recently retired to his newly built bungalow on the outskirts of London, he found living opposite to him a couple living in their bungalow, although it was still in the final stages of completion. Trying to have a friendly word with the man, as he worked around his bungalow, Harold was met with an unpleasant, grumpy reply. The unpleasantness put a blight on the atmosphere of the place, and it saddened Harold, thinking of the man being so unhappy – or why would he behave as he did? But what could Harold do about it anyway, the man was determined to have nothing to do with him? Before going to bed, Harold always stood by his large picture window, gazing out at what he called the 'miracle of the night sky'. There, stretching out endlessly before him, in all its splendour, was the beauty of creation displaying the harmony of the heavens, and on this particular night, he could not suppress a heart-felt cry at the perfection of it all. Then, thinking deeply and sadly about the unpleasant situation around him, in his thoughts he cried out, 'Oh why can't we have such peace, such harmony here on the earth plane?'

The next morning, Harold noticed his grumpy neighbour outside as usual, but it wasn't as usual! The neighbour shouted over to Harold to come and have coffee and taste some home-cooking with himself and his wife; so started a sincere and lasting friendship between the three of them. Could this be a good example of the power of thought?...I would say so.[8]

• • •

Life is ticking along nicely, in fact everything in the garden is 'rosy', 'tickety-boo', to quote two old expressions. We are satisfied, happy with our little lot, then, and out of the blue, something happens and we 'bump the set', another old expression (coal mining)... . Darkness sets in; we didn't see it coming.

In this hectic, frantic, fast moving supersonic world of ours, it seems to be that there are not so many of us who have the time, make the time, or have the opportunity to make the time to sit back, relax, maybe daydream, and think things through. Often those things are: what are we doing? Where are we going? And the best one of all: what's it all about anyway? To realise that, it so often takes a serious upset, a disaster, awful sadness, a seemingly irresolvable situation, before we (and by now in sheer desperation) 'open the door' (we already have the key); open the door, to our inner self. Why? We should all of us who are reading this, by now be making our inner self, our spirit, *part of our everyday life*; asking sincerely for the guidance and help we know is there, waiting for us to simply tune in to; we don't even need to pick up the phone – just make the connection.

'Man possesses a counterpart of the physical body which we call the "spirit body". It is the perfect body, and acts as the vehicle for the spirit self in spirit life, just as our physical body is the vehicle for our material life. The consciousness is the meeting place for both minds.'[9] Words written by Harry Edwards, world famous spiritual healer.

Harry Edwards continues, explaining how, just as the physical mind is in tune with our bodily needs, so the spirit mind can be in tune with thought and guidance from spirit life.

Colour our world? We have it all!

We have it all, in the wonder, the magic – that word again – of the most powerful of ALL the energies, the power of love. It is love that makes the world go round; we are all familiar with that expression (and it has not lasted through the ages for nothing).

The Bible tells us so: 'And now, faith, hope and love abide, these three, and the greatest of these is love.'[10]

The real you, the real me; and, along with the discoveries we make about our world and our true self, comes the understanding (after maybe coming through something tragic, sad, overwhelming) to look at life differently; change our outlook;

and after 'miles' of deep thinking (soul-searching it is called), we know. We see love colouring our world as nothing else can, giving hope, comfort, and strength. Giving us belief that there *is* something/someone out there, caring about us, no matter who we are or what we do; always with us, whatever…and that we are not just destined to travel down a long road to nothingness.

Life now is way ahead with tech! It's going to give us everything, including star ship troopers, the lot, and yet, at the same time, we see glimpses of going back to the past to enlighten the future.

Australia, worried about the seriousness of the bush fire season, where the authorities seemed almost to lose control of the situation, and with the problem not getting any better from year to year, are turning to the natives, the Aborigines, for help. The Aborigines are better at fighting bush fires, and in managing and controlling the land as they always have done, almost like a garden; and on the grasslands with fire breaks.

In America, the Amish community in Pennsylvania, the heart of America, continue to be unyielding to modern-day life, yet their numbers are growing. They avoid the outside world, are reluctant to use many conveniences of modern-day technology, have no electricity, no cars – they use buggies, horses and carriages, or walk. Yet their numbers are growing, and they are one of the fastest-growing religions in America. The Amish community is still as it has always been, with their simple lifestyle and plain dress.

It appears to be that science is looking back for clues to the future, to discover and learn yet more from nature. From the whole of the natural world, there are benefits we could develop for mankind. We are seriously worried at last, and awake to the depletion of our natural resources (we, who have been responsible for the depletion through relentless plundering); now we are trying to make amends as we turn once more to nature for answers.

How truly extraordinary ordinary life is, with nothing certain, and everything possible.

How Was Your Day!

(Thank you for reading.)

Mrs Lambert was a strict but caring woman, always having to dress nicely, always clean and tidy, with everything in place. She was the mother of seven children, grown-up by now and living away from home. They all possessed, as did Mrs Lambert, 'the gift', also known as 'second sight'.

Her husband, Joel Lambert (given as Joe for short), long since dead, had been a soldier in the First World War, and her proudest possession was a photograph of him in his army uniform.

About to start cleaning and decorating, which she did herself, to keep the photograph safe, she put it inside a cupboard, hanging it up inside on the cupboard door, but turning it round so that it faced the door…(if you know what I mean).

Margaret, one of her daughters, lived twenty miles away, on the other side of the river, and knowing nothing at all about her mother's cleaning and decorating escapade, was *more* than amazed when her dead father appeared to her, asking,

"Why has your mother put me in the cupboard?!"

Chapter Seven

The Unbelievable Made Real

> 'While we look not at the things which are seen, but at the things which are not seen: for the things which are seen are temporal: but the things which are not seen are eternal.'[1]
>
> Cor 2 Ch 4 – 18

LIFE, AS WE KNOW, is happening to us all the time; when we are awake, going about our usual affairs, and when we sleep. Thinking about it, however, *do* we sleep? The physical does, but are we, in the so-called sleep state, gently guided into some other reality, dimension, world, from where we have no recall; or *do* we have recall?

Everything touched on in this book is life shouting to us, wanting to grab our attention about the fact that there is So Much More to it than the purely physical (marvellous as it is)! The physical promises throughout life to give us what we can say is 'this and that' until we wake up to the fact that 'we' – you and me, the real you, the real me, are so much more than merely physical beings. When we acknowledge the fact that we are, first and foremost, spirit in a physical body (which we need to inhabit the earth plane), then we really do start to live.

The truth is, that with spirit as our guiding force, and when we know it, there is no 'this and that', but simply, gloriously, EVERYTHING!

(Before I started to write this last chapter, I made a comment to a few friends that 'this chapter is going to write itself'. Judging from the start of it, which you will see for yourself in a minute, it did!)

Leicester: Monday, March 23rd, 2015

Through a strange case of what can only be described as *divine intervention*, I found myself staying at the Mercure Grand Hotel, Leicester, for events leading up to and including – five hundred years after his death – the reburial of the last king of England to be killed in battle (the Battle of Bosworth), King Richard III.

The old Victorian building on Granby Street, Leicester, has no doubt witnessed many exciting times in its long history, but perhaps none more so than now, in this our new world of 2015;

to witness, to be part of, the reburial of a king of England who lived 500 years ago. To repeat the words of Jon Snow, a television commentator of the events, 'you couldn't make it up'. After years of searching, his bones were discovered at last, in an unmarked grave (a thrilling story in itself), discovered through intuition, a strange, strong gut feeling, experienced by Philippa Langley, the leader of what has been described as one of this century's most important archaeological discoveries.[2]

But having mentioned intuition, that strange, strong gut feeling, and there are a few other strange occurrences I would like to share with you in this tale, can I remind you, or pass on to you, a little of the history of King Richard III?

King Richard III was born in 1452, and died in 1485, his name still bearing today, passed down through history, the burden of infamy, infamy in its darkest, cruellest form. However, is this all about to change? Modern technology is leading the way, with experts in every art, in science, history, medicine, having worked together for months to determine the authenticity of the 'find', the skeleton of the king. Scholars, through years of long, hard, research into his life, and therefore his character, hope to find the truth, all of which now points to the fact that he was undeserving of the vile name he had been given by Shakespeare and others all those years ago. He was not deformed, a hunchback as depicted, but had scoliosis, a form of curvature of the spine; he did not have a withered arm and spindly legs; he probably (still awaiting a hundred per cent confirmation but nearly there) did not murder the little princes in the Tower, but would have had them moved for their own safety. All this information is opening up now, five hundred years after his death. The unbelievable made real! You couldn't make it up!

The Battle of Bosworth was where Richard, who was a brave king, fighting side by side with his men, was finally defeated. His battered body was mercilessly hacked, stabbed, and sliced, then stripped naked, bundled over the saddle of a horse (even then having a dagger thrust into his buttocks), to be paraded around the town of Leicester as proof to the people that 'the King is dead'. His body was finally handed over to the friars, who, it seems, hurriedly put him into a makeshift grave; realising that it was too short, they forced his head forward to rest on his chest... so to be found, and confirmed, in our time of 2013, that it really was the remains of King Richard III. Now, five hundred years later, he was to be reburied with all the pomp, the ceremony, the splendour, and the religious rites expected for a King of England; taken into the arms of both the Catholic Church, and the Church of England. King Richard III was reinterred in 2015, in Leicester Cathedral, with full honours, and ceremony, and religious rites. You really could not make it up.

Thursday, the day of the funeral, was a day I decided to spend quietly, watching it on TV in the lounge of the Mercure Grand Hotel, but then something happened...can I tell you about that later? Probably it is best to start at the beginning of the week anyway.

It had been a full, busy week, with so much to see and do, and an air of excitement hanging everywhere. There were white roses in abundance, and candles, and prayer ribbons to tie on railings and happy people, people from all over the world, delighted to be there, enjoying every moment of this unparalleled piece of history. It was a week of talk, conversations bringing in themes like 'intuition', 'fate', 'coincidence', 'chance'. But *could* it have been, simply by chance (and I have my own thoughts about this) that I found myself, on the Monday evening, only hours after arriving – and I should have been somewhere else anyway – standing close to the coffin. People had been queuing for four hours simply to walk past, yet I was so close I could have touched it...the coffin of King Richard III lying in state in Leicester Cathedral.

In awe, in reverence, and in pure amazement, I stood there

quietly, and unhurried, wondering how it had all come about. Without ticket, without pass, without authority of any kind, I was somehow there, right there, in the heart of the 'celebrations', a close part (as if 'folded in') of this unique experience; privileged, blessed by something that I had never even contemplated would happen; something I will never forget.

A full, busy week with various visits – the day at Bosworth Field was a day to remember for its presentation of the history, the story of that dreadful battle, with staff and field guides only too ready to give their all to make the visit as interesting and educational as possible. One coincidence after another (remembering that a coincidence is God's way of working a miracle anonymously) led to meetings that proved the truth of those words. One of them was a little chat with Michael Ibsen, King Richard's closest living relative; a charming, interesting gentleman, quiet, rather shy – and remember that these leading players in the drama had been thrown into the limelight, probably within a matter of weeks. Michael tells the story of a lovely incident that happened as he made the coffin. (He just happens to be an expert carpenter/joiner.) The coffin was made with the best oak to be found from one of the royal estates. One day, as he worked on it, the sun shining through a window, falling straight onto part of the coffin, made it glow like 'pure gold' and he had to rub his hand gently over it to believe what he was seeing.

A conversation with Philippa Langley proved a real treat as she responded so sincerely – and how did *she* keep going? The number of people (including me) who wanted to hear her story was overwhelming yet she responded to the questions about it all patiently, telling it as if for the first time. And what a story, covering not months, but years of hard graft, worry, disappointments, and no doubt, sometimes despair...*and* how strange, how unbelievable (is it really?) that the clincher, the real belter in the saga, was a case of intuition.

Thursday was the day of the funeral, the day I decided to spend quietly, watching it on TV in the lounge of The Mercure Grand Hotel. With no one else around, it seemed that it *would* be quiet, as I sat alone on a long sofa, with my notes and papers, a good half-hour before the funeral service was to begin. A long breakfast bar stood behind me, with about ten bar seats and in front of that, set higher on a wall, was the TV. Cleaning the glass-topped tables, was a young woman called Amy, who kindly came over and offered to put the TV on for me, keeping the sound low until the service began. We chatted for a while about the goings-on in Leicester, and how amazing it all was; the discovery of King Richard's remains, and the thousands of people suddenly there from all over the world. How on earth had it all come about? Then she told me, without any hesitation, of two things that had happened in her home, only the previous day. A can of after-shave lotion had just fallen off a shelf, no one near it, no reason for it to fall. Later, having a meal, she put her knife and fork down, the fork simply lifting itself up to fall on the floor. 'Psychic phenomena,' I said, and she seemed to understand.

Alone again, and with the service about to start, I decided to sit at the breakfast bar, but, just as I was collecting my papers together to make the move, there was the sound of a most terrific crash from somewhere behind me. Startled, I quickly stood up; looking around, all I could see was a metal sheet lying askew, part on the wall, part on the floor, near a corner; could it be from a long radiator which was on the next wall (after the corner)? Then I realised that the radiator was boxed in anyway. Now all was quiet again except for the sound of the TV. The funeral service had just begun.

Amy rushed over, accompanied by one or two male workers from the hotel. Looking more than startled (hair standing on end sort of thing), they made their way over to this metal sheet, carefully, gingerly picking it up to replace it on the wall, next to another. They were obviously a pair; a metal sheet with a picture, 'a print' on the other side. The pictures were of old Leicester, the one that fell was of old buildings with the cathedral towering over them and all along the bottom a row of books by Shakespeare; and in the centre, was a poster, with the words in black, about an inch high, 'The Tragedy of King Richard III.'

We stood, staring at the picture, not saying a word, as if in some hypnotic trance. We all knew that if a picture falls off a wall it falls straight down, not veering two or three yards to the side...

About ten minutes later, left on my own again, and still in a daze, I tried hard to focus on the funeral and not on flying pictures (there *was* only one). I was joined by an American couple who, after exchanging pleasantries, sat next to me at the bar, settling to watch the service. I did not mention pictures! About fifteen minutes after that, a rather burly built man, very smart, in what could have been, I suppose, a day/evening suit, camera in hand, hurried over. He stood, I would say, in an excited state. He was staring at the picture, taking photographs, while muttering words such as 'It can't happen, impossible. This picture could not fall off this wall, it's securely fixed with metal clasps [or clips]; it could not happen, it is impossible.' He glanced towards the Americans who, you remember, knew nothing at all about this (they must have thought he had gone mad). Then, looking towards me, he exclaimed, 'But *we* know that it *did,* don't we?!' Lost for words (for once), I simply, and quietly, answered, 'Yes.' It was later that I found out that the gentleman was the hotel manager. The Americans, so thrilled with the tale when I told them, cautiously glanced at the picture, which was just behind where they were sitting, took photographs and as promised, sent one to me, a reminder, as we agreed, of something special that we had shared.

I wonder what is your opinion of this extraordinary

experience...do you believe that it really could have happened? Do you think that somehow it was engineered or was it true to the title of this book, *The Reality of the Unbelievable?*

• • •

Having just crept into the Age of Aquarius (not so long ago), where, as mentioned in earlier chapters, it is forecast that there will be a Spiritual Revolution at some point (remember also of course that an 'age' can be hundreds, even thousands of years). Thinking about things deeply; life, people, events and reactions – could we not say perhaps, maybe, we are already seeing signs of a spiritual revolution in a gentle, 'not rocking the boat' sort of way. Do we see it in little ways that have already become accepted? For example, instead of saying God, there are a good number of people who talk about or advise putting problems, worries 'out to the Universe'. Instead of saying to someone in trouble (and you want to help, give them some support), 'I will pray for you,' we might use words such as 'I will think about you', 'I will send some thoughts out for you', words that mean the same anyway. And although many of us do not go to church on a regular basis, it seems that we like to attend special services, be part of celebrations (in church), and, dare I say it, we *all* of us love to light a candle as we kneel to a 'superior force' we may not even name (God), but know is there.

In a beautifully written article for *The Sunday Times*, with the heading, 'I can't see God but since my mother's death I can see the value of his house', Camilla Cavendish tells us how, going through life in a sceptical frame of mind with regard to God and religion, full of the 'material' that we really all have to focus on as we go about our daily business, the other side of life, the spiritual, was so often pushed aside. Sometimes scorned, derided, until, one day, 'things in life' happen. They catch up with us; lost, vulnerable, often not knowing where to turn, it is then, as one man so sincerely put it, 'It's at times like these when we realise how lucky we are to have God.'

Camilla's article continues with, 'I can't help wondering what will happen if we edit out all notion of a "higher power"? Do we all become our own little "Gods"?' She ends by wondering what happens to so many of us after the 'storm' has passed. Do we go back to being our usual, old, sceptical selves, or will we, as Camilla is going to do, remind herself 'to be more humble about my own capacity to cope and less passive when the church is under attack. Right now I am thankful it is there.'

Since the beginning, man has always held to a belief in a something, which is an integral part of who we are. Early man focused his belief on nature; the sun, the moon, the planets, which he watched and followed in awe and wonder, consulting through his own devices before every step he made. Generations of history have seen all the changes possible to ways of worship, through wars, revolutions, martyrs, fashion, poverty – we could make an endless list – but through it all, yes, even today, in our twenty-first century, we have not lost the feeling. Trends will come and go, but 'the spiritual nature of man'[3] will always overcome the physical simply because, first and foremost, we are spiritual beings in a physical body, the spiritual taking the lead (of course, not always obvious). Deeply seated is the feeling, the belief, the certainty that there is a higher power, consciousness, reality, a 'something' that is part of our make-up, that is always there; sometimes misunderstood, often neglected or ignored, but there, nonetheless.

Although many people may seem to have problems in general with organised religion, often put off by the style of language, with talk of souls and so on. It *is* true that in today's world, among all the tragedies, disappointments, failures, natural disasters, (horrendous footage shown to us by the media making us more aware), there is an upsurge in giving. Giving (but perhaps not always in money), but giving our time to help through raising money for hard-pressed charities; thinking up all sorts of schemes in sport, entertainment and record-breaking, all to help our fellow man. There is now talk, and quite openly, about how to be really happy; apparently we are at our happiest when we are helping, thinking about others, giving to our time to others, caring. Is this true? What do you think? Now there are organisations set up to help us to help others! True – with headlines such as 'What could be better than helping others?' 'IN KINDNESS, RESPECT, and GENEROSITY… A certain Beauty is Lent to our Lives'. Luke, a young man who has spent the last year doing a good deed every day after a close family friend died of cancer, says, in doing it, 'I feel amazing.'

Communities are pulling together again, not in the same way they did, say, twenty/thirty years ago, but still coming together. The world has changed so much in such a short time but not so long ago, in the mining communities, a certain neighbour would be called upon, and ready, at any time of day or night, to do a 'laying out' after a death; assist at a birth, and there would be neighbours taking turns to sit with someone who was very ill. The community spirit was tremendous, with everybody looking out for everybody else, a sharing and caring still missed today but coming forward again in a different way.

More good news as we hear that 'Young couples send divorce to a 30-year low', another headline pointing to the fact that we are maybe more caring and thoughtful perhaps in how we live. Young people, today's teenagers, are highly aware of social issues, keen to volunteer, and determined to use their digital skills to change society. Teachers who were asked to describe their students, used the words 'caring', 'enthusiastic', and 'hard-working', and according to statistics, research has shown that teenagers are now better behaved. Alcohol and drug abuse among teenagers is falling, and when asked who in the public eye they most respected, the most common response was Nelson Mandela or Barack Obama.[4]

(Now I am reminded of the young woman mentioned at the end of chapter one, who had a large, colourful tattoo on the calf of her leg with the words 'All my hope is in God'. When asked did she believe it, she gave a prompt, positive reply: 'Oh yes.')

Gabrielle Bernstein, a writer, lecturer and coach on new lifestyles, talks about her students being tired of the old ways and selfish attitudes, grabbing the message of the New Age with open arms. She writes – this is from New York but could be anywhere in the world: 'The common issue is a sense of not having a road map, not having an internal guidance system and being disconnected from their "spirituition".' She continues, 'The next generation are looking for a "better way" to live; in love, forgiveness and inner healing.'

• • •

Churches continue playing their part in the community by opening the doors, welcoming in yet more activities of a social nature, going out to the community with 'cafe' churches, involving games and a sit-down meal; communion services in shopping centres, and holding popular services, not only on Sundays but also during the week. A church in the North of England, with the name Hope Church, is asking local people what hurts most or what's the thing in life you find hardest to handle? With regular meetings in the community centre, and response cards (asking the above questions), contact via the media, online, and texting, it seems we have yet another new initiative in place for bringing people together.

A priest, again in the north, enthusiastic about football, and with a big game coming, encouraged fans passing the church on their way to the game to stop by and light a candle!

What are your thoughts, I wonder, on churches staying open

all day and evening, for those who would like to pop in, to say a prayer, light a candle, or maybe just to be there to sit and reflect? I 'am being reminded' that they used to stay open until too many were vandalised or had things stolen. How sad to give way to the selfish wrongdoers – there must be a better way!) We are now being encouraged to take up meditation – and even work places are aiming to set up quiet areas for staff to use. Would it not be possible for churches to do the same, have open doors – some do! After all, surely there is no place quite like a church (or temple or synagogue, or mosque), for leaving all your troubles behind; a place of calm, with a certain inbuilt sense of presence not found anywhere else; a place of safety, comfort, welcome, home – and an escape from the noisy, hectic, busy lifestyle of today.

You could think about, and try to decide whether we are or are not yet in this spiritual revolution forecast aeons of years ago! Is it not a fact that we now talk openly and freely about angels? We talk more freely too about help from the other side of life in times of great distress or trouble, talk openly and freely of experiences that are, without doubt, from an 'un-named' something. We tell of dreams dreamed and messages received…are these things not a sign of something stirring, something changing in our lives? Along with the science and technology (which after all, changes every day), holding up and side by side, maybe even leading the way, is the spiritual. The spiritual is evidenced in something happening, touching our lives, felt, accepted, recognised in part, but perhaps not quite understood. (This reminds me of a well-used remark made by quite a few who hold out against believing: 'I don't believe in anything paranormal or supernatural…but there was – ONE – THING…' There are experiences that are without doubt of an other-worldly nature as they touch lives, never to be forgotten, and often changing everything, even perhaps taking us on the way to accepting the so-called paranormal as the *normal* way of life.

• • •

Steve Tupper, a brave, hardy soldier as he has been (and still is at heart), kindly gave me his story of the fight in the Falklands War for Goose Green. I followed his story by reading the book; Steve, and his wife Lorraine say that he is in good health, and he certainly looks it, but the truth is that it is a miracle that he survived at all, after being shot right through the head. Maybe you would like to read for yourself, parts of the following accounts from the book *Goose Green; a Battle is Fought to be Won.*

Steve was making his way up an incline, near the enemy trenches, when he was wounded, with two bullets to his head. He was to lie, where he fell, for four hours, too far away, and too exposed, for any attempt to get him to be made. Incredibly, he survived, and at last, he was rescued four hours later, when the medics started to clean up and dress his head.

> 'It was a delicate job as much of the top of the skull was shattered. It was like a boiled egg that "had been hit" with a spoon. That he survived was a miracle.'

The book also mentions the Argentines who were held as prisoners; many of them prayed, clutching rosary beads or looking at pictures of the Madonna – something we thought about in an earlier chapter: soldiers at war, and did religion matter?!

Later, Steve, very ill in bed in a hospital, had an OBE (an out of body experience), so real he knows it happened, and although brief, something he will never forget.

The Battle for Goose Green was fought in May 1982, and so, years later, telling me about it, he recounts how he suddenly and to his amazement found himself above the bed, looking down at his body, stretched out, lying there, very still, in a deep sleep. Agitated by this, he could not understand it, thinking, 'How could

I be so lazy?' He remembers coming out with a string of very bad language, aimed at himself to 'get up, you lazy so and so, etc. etc.' He seemed pleased to be able to talk to me about this out of body experience, which had made such an impression on his life, and I was more than pleased to hear about it, so thank you again, Steve.

Out of body experiences, near-death experiences, all are experiences that without doubt are of an other-worldly nature, touching lives, often changing everything.

Ann Sanderson, a retired medical secretary, tells of a childhood near miss, a near-death experience that still haunts her, and it happened over sixty years ago, when she was just two. A sudden noise made her jump with such a start that she fell over the raised cot side and onto the floor. At the same time, she tells us, she had one of the strangest and most lasting memories she has ever experienced.

> 'It was a dream-like scene where I found myself floating high above earth, looking down from outer space. The blackness was all around, highlighting the colours I could see below me – all blues, greens and yellows marking out the countries and seas.
>
> I could see the entire globe so I must have been a long, long way away. There was also a slender, silver cord attached to my left-hand side, reaching all the way back to earth. I felt very tranquil as though it was the most natural thing to be happening, even though I had no idea what I was looking at. This happened in 1951. No colour photographs of the world like that had yet been taken, let alone produced for a toddler to look at, and we didn't even have a black and white television. How could I have known what the earth looked like? I

discovered much later that I'd cracked my collar bone, regaining consciousness in the hospital.'⁶

What an experience, and for a toddler to have! But it was so real, it has remained embedded in her memory, and now she has brought it out into the world for us to share. I am especially interested in her mention of the silver cord.

'Or ever the silver cord be loosed – Eccles 12 – 6-7

Remember the first experience in this book, the young nurse sitting beside a dying patient and witnessing the spirit leaving the body; nurses are encouraged to leave a window open so that the spirit body, once loosed from the physical body (now held by the silver cord), could slip away unhindered to the after-life, the world of spirit.

Experiences, experiences, experiences! We can have one at two years old or one hundred-and-two-years old – anyway, what does age matter, it's only a number? Having a little chat on this subject (experiences), with a doctor (medical), he said, 'I've never had an experience, why have I not had one?' I replied, 'Maybe you have, but you didn't recognise it, you didn't understand.' Experiences, like parables (stories from the Bible), can be so obvious, like the beautifully portrayed story of the widow's mite. Remember that story? Go on, read it up…. Or they can seem as a riddle, a lesson, a message, hidden in a great truth. Shirley looked for evidence of her beloved husband Rick's survival for years. Sometimes she felt she had it, then was not so sure, then again, maybe, and on it went until one day, she had to accept that Rick was indeed still around. The source her evidence came from was unimaginable, but one hundred percent believable.

Shirley's grandson, Sam, suffers from severe autism. Now fourteen years old, he was very close to his grandfather, Rick, who helped with looking after him, and was with him a lot until he passed eleven years ago. Sam cannot communicate very much, and keeps himself engrossed in whatever he is trying to do, or whatever has taken his attention at a particular time. One day, a year or so ago, Shirley called at his home – her daughter's place – to find him busy as usual but, unusually, he looked up at Shirley when she arrived, and managed to say to her, 'Grand-dad Rick here.' Quite taken back, Shirley replied, 'You mean Grand-dad Rick *was* here,' thinking something must have triggered off a memory of his grandfather as he was very close to him. Although it was some years ago now, he still insisted, and was quite emphatic about it, repeating with absolute certainty in his voice as he struggled to reply, 'No, Grand-dad Rick *here.*' This was evidence that came from out of the blue for Shirley, and evidence that was one hundred per cent believable!

Chris, unlike Shirley, who had looked for evidence of her husband's survival (after so-called death), did not know about such things as signs and dreams as evidence that our loved ones, on passing, are not so far away after all. She'd had a sad childhood, not feeling loved or wanted, or knowing the security to be found in a happy, settled, home, but had found it all in her marriage to Baz. They had lived a life full of love and happiness, enjoying life together, in seemingly endless time – as you do – until Baz passed away over fourteen years ago.

'Devastated' is only a word, but the person going through it knows only too well the depth of its meaning, and this was Chris in the years after Baz passed. Over long years, having to work hard, which she agrees was a good thing, and trying to get on with her life, she gradually started to notice that *heart shapes* were beginning to attract her attention and she could not understand why. They made patterns in the movement of the clouds, even the rain lying in a pool, turned into a heart shape; grasses or leaves, patterns made with stones – *anything!* They kept coming to her notice but she gave it no special thought, she just did not understand...until one day something happened that did make her sit up and take notice.

It was breakfast time, when a teabag she had just squeezed out of a cup and laid on a saucer on the kitchen table turned itself into the shape of a heart. This happened right below the photograph of her husband, and on a day that just happened to be a very special day for both of them. And on yet another day, she found her car drenched after a heavy rain storm, the windscreen covered in tiny flowers – all heart shaped. It was as magic to her, and always will be... . She knew then that she had to find out what it all meant.

Chris eventually did find out, coming to accept, to understand, to believe that her husband Baz was still with her, loving her, helping her, and willing her not to be sad – all obvious to those who know about such things, but to Chris, who had not even thought about anything like that before, it was, as she said, 'illuminating', changing her life completely, picking her up to live again, get on with things, be the sort of happy, busy person she had always been, and no doubt still is today.

The things that happen in life, they do make you ponder, wonder, *think*! Experiences are as varied and strange as us humans, thought to be the strangest, most marvellous and most unpredictable of all God's creation.

Olivia Harrison, wife of former Beatle George Harrison, said that when George left his body (passed away), 'There was a light in the room – he just lit the room.' A note he had written on a scrap of paper simply said, 'When you strip it all away, there is only God.'

A father in Germany recently raced to the airport for his son who had forgotten his passport. The son later was killed in an air crash.

'Carol tells us of waking up after a deep sleep, to see a huge orb beside her bed, and it seemed to be full of smoke. After she acknowledged it, it gently lifted away upwards and disappeared. Many orbs are believed to be from spirit – catching up with the new technology, explained and illustrated in *Leaning on the Invisible*.[7]

Katherine says she doesn't understand such things, but has seen flickers of shadows moving around her home as she is sitting quietly. She talks to her husband's photograph every day.

A former FBI employee, sent to the Flight 93 crash site on the 11th September 2001, says she saw angels guarding the scene when she arrived. She has now written a book about her experience.[7]

Pauline, an opera singer, appearing in an opera quartet at a nightclub, in the Midlands, was upset, having just had bad news from home – County Durham, in the north of England. During the interval, a complete stranger approached her to have a chat, and she found herself telling him of her worry. He immediately offered to drive her straight home after the show, and, after a little hesitation, she accepted his offer, thinking it *would* be the quickest and easiest way to get there. True to his word, although it was over one hundred miles, they arrived, safely in the middle of the night, and Jim, without even exchanging names or telephone numbers, as soon as he saw that she was safely in the house, left, making his way back to his home in the Sheffield area.

Years later, wandering alone along busy Oxford Street, London, Jim was taken aback, surprised, amazed, to see

Pauline hurrying by and of course he stopped her, and they had a long conversation, giving Pauline the chance she had always wanted, to thank, once again, this kind stranger. Pauline and Jim married, having many happy years to come to be spent together, always together.

Now we are on to that ever-fascinating, vexing, ever-unanswerable question of fate. Our fate: is everything planned out for us, so we don't have any say in our lives after all???

Sandra tells us a remarkable story as a good example of fate, or what we might think of as fate, but, unlike Pauline's story, that has a happy, romantic ending, this ending is sad.

In 1974, Sandra's mother and sister visited a medium, and during the sitting, they were told, in fact the medium *stressed*, not to buy a petrol-blue car. Despite knowing this (her sister was mad with him), their dad arrived home with a new car, petrol-blue. When challenged as to why he had done such a thing after being warned about it, he just mumbled something like, 'You can't buy a car taking notice of what somebody else says...'

A few months later, as they were preparing to go and open their shop (a fish and chip shop), her dad said, 'Sandra, we'll not take your car today, we'll take mine – the blue one – it needs a run.' It had been standing in the garage for some time. Sandra sat in the back, her mother the front-seat passenger, her dad the driver.

About five miles into the journey, they came to a slight incline in the road – they were behind an oil tanker that had slowed down because of the incline. Her father was impatient; they were a little late to open their shop so he dropped a gear to overtake but as he was overtaking, he saw a van coming in the opposite direction. With not enough room for the three of them, he started to turn in front of the oil tanker, then, starting to slow down, he moved back in, the back of the car clipping the tanker...the weight of the oil tanker turned the car over, to land on its roof, facing the wrong way. Sandra and her dad got out. As she said, 'OK,' the door burst open and her mother fell out. She was dead.

Fate; as we have thought about it in an earlier chapter, perhaps we need not pursue the subject any further here, except to read again a few of the beautiful words from the Bible, Ecclesiastes.

'To everything there is a season, and a time to every purpose under the heaven: a time to be born, and a time to die: a time to weep, and a time to laugh.'

Could it be that there really is our very own special time to be born, our very own special time to die, but that we ourselves fill in the rest? Free will…but with a divine, guiding hand all the way – *if* we take notice and listen!

Scientists, philosophers, and indeed most deep-thinking people appear to have come to the conclusion that there really is a 'something' out there. Not always understood, intangible, yet can be tangible, illusive, but very much a presence, it is often unexplainable and while just at the point of shouting 'Eureka! it answers with yet more questions than ever answers could be found.

The world is not only moving *towards,* but there are many indications that the world is now at the *beginning* of the spiritual revolution, forecast to happen in this, The Age of Aquarius. The Age of Aquarius is also called The New Age, where we move on to what has been called 'The Fifth Dimension', which means, to put it simply, the earth plane lifted spiritually onto a higher vibration, with the consciousness of people turning to a more spiritual outlook in life, instead of focusing so much on materialism.

This move, or change, is evidenced throughout the book, as we see positive signs of shifts in attitudes and behaviour towards not only each other (humanity) but to our beautiful world. Conservation is now a key word, and acted upon, with new *understanding* and *feelings* and *help* spilling over into the animal kingdom, including wildlife sanctuaries in the Arctic, elephant sanctuaries in India, a hospital exclusively for birds in Delhi, signs springing up everywhere of the new concern and care for *all* nature.

The numbers of wildlife are rising (including the numbers of lions). And we hear of cat and dog shelters being inundated with people forming queues, taking old sheets and blankets and cushions and pillows and Christmas treats to ease the dreadful plight of some domestic animals. So it would appear that *we,* you and me, and after all, we are the world, are heading, at last, in the right direction. Hallelujah!

The world is turning (not only literally); we are all, gradually turning to accept, to recognise that spirit, the world of spirit, is no fantasy island but is what drives, gives breath to the physical, to human and animal, nature, all spheres of life. It is the energy to which we are all bound; the words of one enlightened being, telling us to, 'Walk in the light of the true, invisible reality, the Spirit, to guide us through any, and all situations.' And can I add, to develop our talents (we all have them), to find the best in life. Be positive; always have hope, knowing we are loved beyond our understanding. Be kind; listen to the inner self – our very own inner self – the inner, the 'something' that calls out to us, the invisible reality, the spirit, keeping us in check, encouraging, pointing out to us the way of happiness; giving us strength in the hard times that we all go through.

Anthony loved life. He cared about people, putting his Christian values into practice by helping others whenever he could, and this while he himself was often in pain. He suffered throughout his life as the result of accidents and poor health, yet he was always a positive, happy man. He could be mischievous (not in a bad way), loved a laugh and a bit of fun; was interested in many things, and was a talented watercolour artist. Loving to be out and about, always immaculately dressed, not everyone realised his quieter self – his inner strength, his faith, as he faced his on-going health problems with fortitude and dignity, never complaining. His inner strength was visible in the way he lived and confirmed in the way he died…saying, with his last breath to the loved ones gathered around him, and to the minister present, 'The best is yet to come.'

Our way of life is changing fast, but one thing that will never change, is the fact that we are spiritual beings, here and now, in a physical body, living on the earth plane. Perhaps it will be seen as a contradiction to the highly technical, materialistic, times we appear to be so fully immersed in; however, it appears to be that the spirit, our inner self, is being encouraged, and pushed forward more now than ever! Talks, information, even in the workplace, on how to be healthy and happy: much encouragement is given to us to walk as much as possible, exercise as much as possible, take up yoga, meditate or have a quiet time. The Royal Horticulture Society is about to launch a new, more comprehensive campaign extolling the virtues of gardening, intended to help those who would like to start their own garden, or even a window box. Help is there, with groups being set up all over the country for anyone, any age, to join and experience the joy of being outdoors, close to nature, pleasantly involved in one way or another, and socially, a good thing too! There is no need to be lonely with the many varieties of interests that are covered, so much choice, in clubs, groups, and evening classes.

Have you noticed the adverts that are full of advice on how to live and be happy; 'do this' 'take that', again, our inner self is often seen as a target for products to make us more buoyant, or calmer, or more relaxed, while even a famous jeweller advertises his gems with the message, 'Reveal the Beauty Within.'

The media seem to be forever asking us to think these days, to send in ideas, opinions, preferences, with audience participation on the rise – as a reward?

Philosophies of life are constantly appearing on walls such as in shopping malls, but nowadays we could expect them to turn up anywhere, with snippets of advice (they could be sermons) such as:

> 'Life is full of twists and turns – like a roller coaster. We have our highs and lows, but we hang on.'
> 'Do to others what you would have them do to you.'
> 'Life is about finding yourself.'
> 'Life is about creating yourself.'
> 'Love what you do.'

Texts, sayings, many of them are very funny…

> 'I was happy for twenty-five years, then I met you.'
> 'A man is not complete until he is married, then he's finished!'

Many of the texts, sayings, are deeply thoughtful, focusing on the inner;

> 'Who looks outside dreams,
> Who looks inside wakes.'

We have another surprising contradiction in our world today, as modernity offers us a recipe for ill health, with the constant advertising of junk food for a faster way of life, and now a serious worry – what to do about an obesity epidemic, not only in this country, but what seems to be a problem worldwide.

We have the best of transport to offer; more cars than ever before, with some of them, in the not too distant future, to be driverless (and we are supposed to be trying to free our already tangled, over-crowded roads!). Yet we are often held immobile at home as we lie – a couch potato? – Or we sit, glued to a monitor (screen) of one kind or another; screens getting smaller and multiplying by the day (or hour), and all this is 'good for us'; progress, the New Age.

Sarcasm apart, and of course we have countless excellent things going for us in this our new age, but through all the distractions, the changes, the problems, helping us, guiding us, in, as some would say, this crazy world of ours, ever faithful, always present, is spirit.

• • •

This writing has just taken a surprising turn for me. Struggling with this, the last part of the last chapter, with a mixture of sadness that it is coming to an end, I have a concern that I am going on too much about our spirit, our inner life and so on. Still thinking about this, as I got up this morning, I turned the radio on in time to hear the news, and was just in time to hear the last few words of an interview with an American author, whose new book apparently focuses on our inner life, our spirit, and a worry that it is now being neglected, overlooked. He is a very wealthy, successful entrepreneur (extremely wealthy, *he* stressed), but the important thing in life, as he says, is that we must try to get back to regaining our inner life, the life that gives us a gentleness of nature, a caring nature, a purpose. The spiritual side of us is what lends a 'something' – gives a shine, a beauty, a radiance, depth, character, to our lives, bringing kindness in all we do.

He ended by saying, 'Yes, of course have a great career, but having a great inner life is everything.'

My spirit lifted as I flew to find pen and paper and scribble down the words as he spoke, and later, I thought how lucky I was to have heard them, these words of a like-minded author, for me to be there, just at that moment – another moment or two and he would have been and gone. Was it luck, or chance, or a coincidence that I was there? A coincidence (as we know) is God's way of working a miracle anonymously. What do you think?

An old saying we thought about in an earlier chapter:

> People may not remember what you say or do,
> but they will never forget how you made them feel.'

How you made them feel.

Those words are the essence, the heartbeat of our innermost being; who we are, with all our faults and weaknesses, you and me. It is about our feelings, emotions, intuition, that inspiration, Conscience (raw and remorseful as it sometimes is). It is *our innermost being* accepting and believing in the reality of the world of spirit. And as we understand and accept, keeping ourselves open and receptive to the messages, the guidance, the evidences we are sure to receive – Ask and it shall be given you; seek and you shall find – so will we see the promise of a prophet, a teacher, a seer, fulfilled.

While we look not at the things which are seen, but at the things which are not seen.[8]

> The Kingdom of God is not coming with things that can be observed,
> Look, here it is! For in fact, the Kingdom of God is within.[9]

The Reality of the Unbelievable
Our Spiritual Revolution…
The New Age.

Mary Bowmaker

References

*The Religious Experience Research Centre, University of Wales, Ceredigion, will be referred to as RERC in the references.

Chapter One

Setting the Scene

1 RERC, no 002715.
2 Sir George Trevelyan, *Selected Lectures*, 'Awakening Consciousness'.
3 The Aura, *Leaning on the Invisible*, Mary Bowmaker, p72.
4 Lynne McTaggart, *The Field*, prologue, p296.
5 Letter from Oslo, *Sunday Telegraph* Feb 2012.
6 Matthew 1-24.
7 Judges 13-8.
8 Psalm 91-11.
9 Luke 1-37.
10 Acts 12 7-9.
11 Hebrews 13-2.
12 Acts 9-7.
13 Exodus 14-16.
14 Luke 19 – v1-10.
15 *Is anybody there...* Mary Bowmaker, p16.
16 RSPB slogan.
17 *Leaning on the Invisible*, Mary Bowmaker, p174/5.
18 'All my hope is in God', Isaiah 40-41.

Chapter Two

We are Two Worlds

1 *Is anybody there...* p1 Mary Bowmaker.
2 Luke 11 – 9.
3 President Obama, *The Audacity of Hope.*
4 *Frequency*, Penny Peirce, p25.
5 In 1943 the 'Dickin Medal' instituted to honour the contributions of all animals in conflict.
6 Ralph Waldo Emerson, 1802-1882.

Chapter Three

Divine Transportation

1 Rosemary Brown, *Immortals By My Side*. First published in England in 1974 by Bachman & Turner, London, under the title *Immortals at my Elbow.*
2 Samuel 1 3-3.
3 RERC, no 004410.
4 Composer John Tavener, *Psychic News*, chief reporter Kay Hunter.
5 Dr Penny Sartori, *The Wisdom of Near-Death Experiences*, Watkins Publishing.
6 Matthew 7-12.
7 Luke 2 v12.
8 Matthew 2 v10.
9 Matthew 2 v12.
10 Chronicles 5 v12 – 14.

Chapter Four

An Awakening of Understanding

1 Luke ch 11 v9, 10.
2 *Daily Mirror,* 2011, Cancer Smart Bomb.
3 A Human Consciousness – for further reading on this subject, *The Aquarian Conspiracy,* Marilyn Ferguson, *The Awakening Earth,* Peter Russell.
4 Isaiah 9 – 2.
5 *Cold,* Ranulf Fiennes, p361, pub Simon & Schuster 2013.
6 Psalm 46 v1.
7 Flight MH 370 Not found, despite a worldwide search – assumed it ended in the southern Indian ocean.
8 *The University of Spiritualism,* p187, Harry Boddington, *Psychic News.*
9 Thessalonians ch 5 v18.
10 Romans ch 8 v28.
11 Ralph Waldo Emerson 1803-1882.
12 *Meditations,* Marcus Aurelius 121 – 180.
13 In *Tune with the Infinite,* R W Trine, p66.
14 *Ibid* p70/71.
15 *Ibid* p70.

Chapter Five

The Complete (Total) Self

1 *Tommy: The British Soldier on the Western Front 1914-1918,* p241, Richard Holmes, Harper Collins 2004.
2 *The Sunday Times,* Feb 2014, Mark Hookham Defence Correspondent.
3 Angel of Mons – *Is Anybody There...* p64, Mary Bowmaker.

4 Luke 16 10 – 22.
5 Samuel 1 16 – 7.
6 Luke 1 – 37.
7 Eccles 11 – 1.
8 Eccles 9 – 11.
9 Psalm 91 v11.
10 Romans 8 – 28.
11 John 6 – 63.
12 From a poem by Alfred Lord Tennyson.

Chapter Six

Colour My World

1 *The Interconnected Universe*, Ervin Laszlo.
2 *The Field*, pxiv, Lynne McTaggart.
3 *The Quantum Dream Dictionary*, Pamela Ball.
4 *The Sunday Times*, 'Arctic Wild Life Refuge', January 2015.
5 Deepak Chopra, author.
6 *The University of Spiritualism*, p96, Harry Boddington.
7 'Aurora Borealis', cruise on the mail ship *Hurtigruten*, Norway.
8 Harold Sharp, *Is anybody there...* p119, Mary Bowmaker.
9 Words written by Harry Edwards, the most famous spiritual healer of our time in his book, *Spirit Healing*, p20, pub Burrows Lea, Shere, Surrey.
10 Corinthians 1 13 – 13.

Chapter Seven

The Unbelievable Made Real

1 Corinthians 11 ch 4 – v18.
2 *BBC History Magazine*.

3 Sir Alister Hardy book title (RERC publication).
4 *The Sunday Times* 2014/15.
5 *Goose Green*, Mark Adkin, pub 1992 by BCA by arrangement with Pen & Sword Limited.
6 *Daily Mail*, January 2014.
7 *In the Shadow of a Badge*, a spiritual memoir by Lillie Leonardi.
8 Corinthians 11 ch 4 v18.
9 Luke 17 v20/21.